THROUGH AN

EASTERN

WINDOW

THROUGH AN
EASTERN
WINDOW

JACK
HUBER

St. Martin's Press
New York

To the late Ishiguro Horyu Roshi
of Tokyo
and the Mahasi Sayadaw
of Rangoon

CHAPTER I

IT WAS IN JANUARY when I began to take the idea seriously.

Four years before, I had taken a trip around the world, and it was then that the whole thing began to take shape in my mind. On that trip I saw every psychological institution and spoke to every professional person in the psychological fields I could find. Before I left the United States at that time I had asked everyone I knew and some people I did not know for letters of introduction to Far Eastern professional people. I left with one or two letters.

Very few people in the West seem to know people in the East, let alone understand their ideas and points of view. In one way or another, through one person telling me about another person, I eventually visited colleges, clinics, and hospitals, and spoke with both students and professional people in psychology, psychiatry and social work.

What I discovered was this: the Eastern psychological professions have adopted not only the Western scientific methodology but the subject matter and techniques as well. I could see almost nothing uniquely Eastern about what they were doing. They were performing our kinds of experiments, using our testing procedures, diagnosing according to our categories and administering therapy with our methods. Nothing of what they were doing, so far as I could see, originated with them. We had, it appeared to me from my modicum of observation, taken over the initiative in producing almost all psychological ideas and practices for the Eastern nations.

They seemed to be taking from us and offering nothing. Or perhaps, I began to think, there was something in their attitudes, in the way they *used* our ideas and techniques, that I could not see unless I lived there for some years or at least had some intimate training there. Perhaps there was a factor in their work deriving from their philosophies or religions which I could not know about.

Or perhaps there was something in the Far East which might broaden and enrich psychology in both the East and West if it could be ferreted out.

I had had hints of these possibilities only in my visits to two institutions. During that summer I had visited a Zen psychiatric hospital. There I had been shown the institution and had had a chance to see how the patients were treated.

The patients were put into private rooms where they were completely alone for days on end. They were provided no stimulation through books or anything else. There was no contact with anyone except for a five-minute interview with the therapist each day. Even when meals were brought, the tray was quickly slipped into the room and the patient did not speak to the bearer. The patients were told to focus their attention on their sufferings and whatever else went through their minds. The patient was forced to live completely alone with himself and his sufferings and could complain to no one.

I had thought about this treatment, but I could see only its seemingly vast difference from Western treatment — the seclusion, the lack of discussion and analyzing, the emphasis on living with the suffering rather than complaining about, analyzing, or trying to avoid it. Here at least was something new to me, something different from the practices familiar to me in the West. To the best of my knowledge this hospital was not well known to Japanese psychologists and psychiatrists. They apparently were busy learning Western methods and took little interest in any new Eastern ideas.

Something else from the hospital kept recurring in my mind. During our conversation, the chief psychiatrist told the following story.*

A Buddhist nun had been sent from a nunnery in the countryside of Japan to do shopping in the nearby large city. She had never been in a large city before. Her buying accomplished, she returned to the nunnery. In a short time the other nuns noticed her behaving strangely, and when she became acutely disturbed she was put to bed. The major symptom was her terror at the snakes she saw crawling over her body. Physicians and then psychologists and psychiatrists were brought to see her but they could do nothing for her. Finally a Zen psychiatrist, famed in the big city, was brought in. He was in her room for only five

* I am indebted to Dr. Shin-ichi Usa, Sansei Hospital, Kyoto, Japan, for this story. The Zen psychiatrist in the story was Dr. Usa's father. I hope I have quoted the story correctly.

minutes. "What is the trouble?" he asked. "The snakes, the snakes crawl over my body and frighten me." Perhaps she let out a scream as a snake crawled over her. The psychiatrist thought a bit and then said, "I must leave now, but I shall come back to see you in a week. While I am gone, I want you to do two things. First, complain to no one. Say nothing more of this matter to anyone. And second, observe the snakes very carefully so that when I return you will be able to describe their movements accurately to me." In seven days he returned and found the nun out of bed and doing the duties she had been assigned before her illness. He greeted her and then asked, "Did you follow my instructions?" "Indeed," she answered, "I complained to no one. And then I centered all my attention on the snakes. But alas, I saw them no more, for when I observed them carefully they were gone."

I was intrigued with the story. I must say that I made two assumptions: that the psychiatrist's actions helped the nun and that his actions had something to do with keeping her functioning over the years. These are the common and often unrecognized assumptions we make about psychotherapy. I had known of Western therapists who occasionally do very short-term treatment involving actions not totally dissimilar from the Zen psychiatrist's action, but I never had the idea that the Westerners' actions were based on any deep convictions with some theoretical or philosophical base. I did have the feeling that the Zen approach was well thought out and that the treatment was firmly grounded in theory or philosophy. My training as a psychologist did not allow me to understand their theory. I felt I would have to engage in personal Zen practice before I could understand.

Later that summer I was in Delhi where I was given an interview with the leading Yoga teacher in that city. In our two hours together I was told about students learning to control bodily functions which I would never have dreamed could be controlled to such an extent. Furthermore he hinted that thoughts and attitudes were controlled by long discipline training, not as in the West by discussions of personal problems.

Perhaps, I thought, there *were* points of view and techniques of a different nature from ours, but they were rare and not well known to psychology in either the East or West.

I could see no way to get close enough to these points of view to judge them or incorporate them into my framework. I was years away from a sabbatical leave of absence from my university. Even if I found some kind of training, I would have only a summer to give to it. I read some Zen literature, but I could not see myself getting any Zen training in part of a summer. Yoga training, I assumed, also required many years of deep and concentrated involvement.

To add to the interest stimulated by these experiences, I also felt there might be something for me in the Far East beyond a professional enrichment. I had read just enough of Zen to feel that something was there which might be meaningful to me as an individual and even perhaps as a psychologist.

My life was going fairly well. I had a job which had

great meaning and stimulation for me; I had deeply satisfying relationships with people; my life was fairly creative. I
had always had the feeling that I lived, so to speak, in the
best of all possible worlds. And yet I never felt I was really
getting the most satisfaction possible from it. Perhaps
there was more to appreciate, some more totally involved
way to live, and perhaps I was not seeing it. Perhaps there
was something the Far Easterners had to tell me. But I
could see no way to get to it.

And then in January I read Admiral E. H. Shattock's
An Experiment in Mindfulness. Here was a book about a
Westerner — neither a professional philosopher nor a psychologist — a literate, down-to-earth, educated man, who
had taken three weeks out of his life to engage in meditation training in Burma, and he seemed to have learned
something from it. The training was rigorous, solitary, and
so unusual in many ways that I found it hard at first to
imagine my doing it. I kept thinking about it.

Finally in April I wrote to the Meditation Center in
Burma asking if I could come for three weeks as Shattock
had done. I received a prompt reply. Their letter was
typewritten on formal stationery with "The Ven'ble
Mahasi Sayadaw" printed at the top. The letter stated:

> We shall gladly welcome you as a pupil for Satipat-
> thana course. The course at our center will vary from
> a minimum of six weeks to ten weeks, depending on
> the progress of the pupil. We wish you can stay with
> us at least six weeks, so that you may be able to achieve
> good results. We do not think that three weeks' time

is adequate, but if you are prepared to undergo an intensive training, your short stay will have served a useful purpose, in that you can continue your exercises on your return home, and reach the desired end in due course.

As to expenses during your stay at the Center, you will have to pay about Kyat 10 to 15 [about 2 to 3 dollars] a day for your meals. Accommodation is provided free of charge.

If you are arriving around 25th July, you will have raining season awaiting you — fine and cool.

It was signed "With loving kindness. Yours in the Dhamma, Mahasi Sayadaw."

I read the letter over repeatedly. Intensive training. I wondered what *that* meant. Did he mean it would be more rigorous than Shattock's training? I began to have doubts about going. No, I was sure I could not do it. Yes, if he did it, I could do it. Back and forth. Finally I decided to write Admiral Shattock for encouragement. Being a Westerner, he would understand my ambivalence and indecision. I wrote him a short note saying that I had been accepted for training but was doubtful about going. He wrote back immediately. What he said was:

I was delighted to get your letter and to hear that you have decided to undergo the Satipatthana training. I don't think you need have any fears; there is nothing difficult about it provided you are prepared for the monotony and the seclusion.

The limitation of the period to three weeks presents a difficulty simply because you will tend to have this time limit in your mind, and apparent lack of success may make you impatient. You will have to try and forget that there is an end always in sight and work for the moment only. You must try to develop an attitude of patient persistence, not caring about slow progress but intent on *guiding* your mind to stillness. I don't think the Sayadaw meant that your training would have to be stricter than mine, but you will have to resist all interruptions. I found that visitors, mostly inquisitive, had to be discouraged.

I envy you your opportunity. You will find the training of immense value even if you don't manage to achieve Samadhi which is the balanced state without thought. You will, of course, find it easier if you have had any previous experience of meditation, but that isn't necessary.

More ambivalence. I was somewhat encouraged by his letter, but I had fleeting thoughts about the possible differences between us as men. I could see him in the navy for years, doing solitary night watch on the bridge. Solitude was probably his usual life condition. I was highly gregarious. I had learned in years of psychoanalysis that I use human contact, often indiscriminately, to escape my problems and to avoid facing myself.

Should I go to Burma? Yes, I would go. Too much was at stake. I had the chance of having an experience which, at a minimum, could enlarge my professional viewpoint.

And I had the even greater chance of seeing something of a personal nature which might expand my appreciation of the world. I wrote to Burma saying I would come for three weeks. I even began to tell myself there was no doubt about my sticking it out.

About the same time, through a letter from a Japanese psychologist I had met on my previous trip, I learned of a Zen course in Tokyo. I had no idea what it was all about but my informant had said in his short letter that the attempt of the course was to get a "glimpse into one's own nature." I liked the phrase, but I had no idea what he meant by it, and I was sure he could not, or would not, elucidate.

With no hesitation at all I wrote to the Zen master and asked for admission to his school. The immediate reply was typewritten on plain white paper with nothing at the top except the date.

> I am most happy to inform you that it will be my great pleasure to give you guidance in Zen practice.
>
> The next Zen training will begin on the 13th of June and end on the 17th which is for five days. I shall appreciate your presence at the school at 6:00 p.m. of the 12th as I have arranged to have an interpreter to explain to you the fundamentals of my training.
>
> I am looking forward to meeting you.

It was signed, "With warmest regards. Sincerely yours. Horyu Ishiguro."

Having become accustomed to the idea of three weeks of solitary confinement in Burma, I felt five days was almost no threat at all. I could stand anything for five days. It was another rare chance for a professional experience. I do not believe I had any hopes of personal enrichment from only five days. I knew Zen training required many years.

So on June 10, I left New York City for Tokyo and the Zen school. From Tokyo I went to Hong Kong, Kuala Lumpur and Penang in the Malayan States, Bangkok, and then the Meditation Center in Rangoon, Burma. The rest of the summer I spent in India, some of the cities in the Middle East, Barcelona, London. I returned to New York on September 9. And something had happened to me.

CHAPTER II

I HAD NO IDEA what I was getting into.

I arrived in Tokyo on June 10 at a little after midnight following a fourteen-hour flight in a race with the sun. I had been told that two or three days would pass before my system adjusted to the insult of leaving New York at 5:30 P.M. and arriving in Tokyo after midnight the same evening, on the Japanese calendar one day later and in time fourteen hours later. The plane trip was in my mind a matter of a long evening — I began Martin Buber's *I and Thou*, talked to the other two people sitting beside me, drank a cocktail and ate dinner with them, stopped for a look at Anchorage, Alaska, read some more, slept a little, and I was in Tokyo. Despite my feeling that I had had a normal evening, I had really had a full day of preparation in New York plus fourteen hours of more anticipation and excitement than I recognized.

At about 1:00 A.M. I registered in the teeming, metropolitan Dai Ichi Hotel in the center of Tokyo, requested a room with a view, and was taken to a small room high up in the hotel. I immediately went to the window, pulled the curtains apart, and saw before me a large section of Tokyo. Almost directly under the window were train

tracks and, as I watched, a train passed. I opened the case-
ment, wanting to feel I was in direct contact with what I
saw, and began unpacking. I hung up my one suit and
extra jacket and slacks, put my few other things in drawers,
and went to the bathroom and brushed my teeth. By about
2:00 A.M. I was in bed. As I lay there, I heard another
train pass with a great roar and I got up and closed the
window. I have no trouble sleeping under almost any conditions, but the sound was loud.

I awakened wide-eyed two hours later. I lay in bed
thinking I would fall asleep again, but gave it up as a lost
cause. I went to the window again, opened it for the air
and the view. I realized I had felt closed up and was glad
to be in contact with the view again. The trains passed
and the room was intermittently filled with their noise. I
shaved, brushed my teeth again, washed a pair of socks,
looked out of the window again, wrote a couple of post-
cards I had picked up on the plane — anything to make
the time pass. I was sure the dining room would be open at
seven and I thought seven would never come. Keeping
myself busy in the tiny room was a hard job, but seven
finally showed itself on my watch and I went downstairs.
The dining room door was shut; breakfast was served at
eight. I busied myself again. I looked in the lobby showcases, sat down in one of the lobby chairs, got up, looked in
more showcases.

After what seemed to be hours, the dining room doors
opened. I sat down to eggs, bacon, toast and coffee. I felt
good again. I was among people and things were busy
and active.

The next two days were filled with the same kind of busy activity. I found myself thinking with no progress about the Zen school. Since I did not know what I would be doing there, I was a little nervous about it, but I did want to get there and see what it was all about.

And now two days later, still in something of a confused and excited state, I was riding in a taxi with a solicitous driver searching for the meditation center of a Zen master. The house was not easy to find, and the driver had to leave the cab three times to ask where the house was located, always explaining to me with gestures and Japanese words that I was to remain in the cab. I had given him a slip of paper on which was written the address in Japanese; desk clerks in Japanese hotels do that favor for visitors. We went from wide streets to narrow roads and eventually to small lanes barely able to accommodate the tiny Japanese cab. The driver got out for the last time at a gate, opened the cab door for me, smiled proudly and indicated that he had been successful in his assignment — I was where I had said I wanted to be.

The cab driver carried my bags to the front door of the center, bowed, got in his cab, looked again and smiled, and left. I knocked on the door at almost exactly 6:00 P.M., the hour appointed for the beginning of my training. As I stood waiting, I wanted to peek into the building. There was no small window in the door to look through, no clear windows on this side of the house. In fact no view at all to give a hint of what to expect.

No sound of footsteps came, but suddenly the door opened.

I faced a very small man of indeterminate age, completely bald, dressed in a brown, somewhat transparent robe worn over a white robe of heavier fabric. He smiled broadly, nodded, but did not speak. I guessed he was the master. We bowed and smiled and I gave my name. I deposited my bags on the flagstone floor just inside the doorway, and he watched as I took off my shoes before walking up the one step to the wooden floor. I put on guest slippers and did not realize that with one exception I would not again use my own shoes until I was ready to leave the school.

He continued to smile as he showed me into a small room to the right of the front hall. A round table was in the center of the room. Three armchairs of 1930's "modernistic" design were placed around the table and the master indicated by gesture that I should sit down across from him. This was the central room of the house through which I would be passing countless times with countless moods — discouragement, self-incrimination, boredom, affection.

When we had seated ourselves, the master and I looked at each other. He smiled, grew serious for a moment in what seemed to be a desire to find English words, smiled again. We were not permitted to continue this beyond a minute or two; the doorbell rang. The master got up, went into the hall, and returned with a young Japanese woman in Western dress. She was of the height and weight of an average American woman, not of the fragility I had grown accustomed to seeing in Japanese women. Her English was quick and more American than British.

We introduced ourselves and talked for a few minutes while the master watched. She had been to college and graduate school in the United States and now taught speech in a Tokyo college. She had also been an interpreter and a teacher of interpreters. She explained that she would try to translate in a literal way what the master would say. The master began to speak of Zen. In the middle of interpreting she would turn to me and say, "I don't understand what that means. Perhaps I have not translated it well. Do you understand?"

Did I understand? What he said had meaning to me. I did not want to get into a discussion; I wanted to hear what the master had to say. I left the matter with, "I understand."

Then there was another interruption. One I had not expected. The doorbell rang again, and another Westerner, a man of sixty years or so, was shown into the room. We introduced ourselves and I immediately began to wonder if I would have to share a room with him. I wanted to be alone, but I could not imagine that this seemingly small house would provide private rooms for the two of us and the other students as well. Actually I had no idea of how many students there would be.

I glanced around and was surprised to see through another door of the room a Japanese boy of perhaps eighteen years sitting on the floor in Japanese fashion with legs under him. He never looked up nor did he attempt to come into the room. He sat mute, listening to the master's words at a short distance from the Westerners. The next day I discovered that he was a new student like myself.

I wish I could repeat verbatim what the master said, but I could not write it down. I was too busy listening. The essence of the conversation, however, is clear in my mind. He said that in the five days the attempt would be to gain a "glimpse into one's own nature." We live "conditionally" through our "conditional nature." Our attempt in the five days would be to see our "unconditional nature." He proudly handed us a small booklet written in Japanese by him and translated into English. We were to read it later.

As the master spoke, the other Westerner interrupted intermittently and attempted to relate or compare the master's comments to a philosophical or psychological idea of his own. "I see," he would say, "that's like what I teach," or, "Oh yes, we do the same thing." The master would nod when the Westerner spoke, and then he would proceed. I was irritated; I did not want to hear a discussion. I wanted only to hear the master speak and wanted no comparisons or interpretations.

The master listed the "conditions of success" in our five-day training. There were six:

1. Concentrate on the Buddha nature.
2. Concentrate on the counseling of the dokusan (private interview with the master).
3. Cooperate and help one another in every way possible so that everyone in the group may succeed. Say nothing to interfere with another's progress, nothing to upset him.

4. Never hesitate to give your effort, give all you can, throw yourself into it so that there is no reserve.
5. Observe the rules and regulations strictly.
6. Keep your mind blank. Be ready, trustful and honest.

These six conditions had little meaning to me at the time, mostly because (with the exception of the first condition which I did not understand) I had no choice but to act as he prescribed. I had every intention of following the rules. I would cooperate fully and had no desire to interfere with anyone else. I could be nothing but trustful since up to now I had heard no ideas to be untrustful about. I would probably throw myself into it; friends make a joke of my enthusiasm. At least for the moment my mind was open if not blank; I knew nothing of what I was getting into.

The rules and regulations he referred to were in essence a list of prohibitions:

1. Do not read during the five days.
2. Do not talk unless absolutely necessary.
3. Take an hour's nap after each meal.
4. Do not leave the house.
5. Do not talk about the private interview with the master.

The prohibitions were no surprise to me. My visit to the Zen mental hospital four years before had prepared me for the Zen emphasis on no outside stimulation through reading or talking. The nap made no sense to me. Not talking about the private interview was a natural prohibition to me; therapists often prescribe the same prohibition to patients.

The master got up from his chair, walked over to the wall, removed a hanging placard, and brought it to the interpreter. She read to us our daily schedule:

5:30 Getting up and washing
Zazen (meditation)
6:30 Dokusan (private teaching or interview)
Dokyo (reading sutras — parts of Buddhist scriptures)
Breakfast
One hour sleep
8:00 Zazen
11:30 Dokusan
Lunch
One hour sleep
1:30 Zazen
3:00 Tea — followed by Zazen
4:30 Dokusan
Supper
One hour sleep
6:30 Zazen
8:30 Dokusan
Tea
Go to bed

I had no notion that I might as well have been reading,

"You will stand on your head for eight hours, to be followed by putting your head in a vice for twelve, then your legs will be crushed for eighteen hours. During this time you must go to sleep exactly on schedule, sleepy or not. A total of sixty-four hours each day. That is all." The schedule seemed impossible but still not as formidable as the Burmese one described by Shattock. I again consoled myself that I could stand anything for five days.

The master motioned us to rise and follow him. We left the wooden floor of the central room, removed our slippers and entered in stockinged feet on to the tatami (a kind of woven straw) floor of the adjoining room. No furniture except one low, round table. Cushions for sitting were piled in a corner. In a niche hung a scroll. The interpreter explained that this was the bedroom to be used by the two Westerners.

At the far end of the room was a small porch as wide as the bedroom and about three feet in depth. The width of it consisted of two sliding doors made of glass, the top half clear and the bottom half opaque. I walked slowly to the glass doors and looked through them. A small, neglected Japanese garden was outside. There were trees and shrubs but obviously no one had paid much attention to them recently. I later found no one had time to produce the usual delicate, manicured Japanese garden. The garden was enclosed by a wall and beyond the wall were railroad tracks. As I looked out, a large suburban train passed, accompanied by an ear-shattering train whistle. The ground and the house shook. This was where we would sleep.

As I stood looking out of the glass doors the master appeared noiselessly beside me. He smiled and I returned his smile. Then his brows knitted; he wanted to say something to me. He pointed to the lower panes of the glass doors; opaque.

"You see? . . . you see through?" he asked in faltering English. I shook my head. He smiled for a second then pointed to the clear upper panes.

"You see through?"

"Yes," I replied.

Pointing to the opaque glass, he said, "Conditional nature," and pointing to the clear glass, "Unconditional nature." Then, "Put together," and he put the palms of his hands together as in a prayer gesture and bowed to me. "Put together . . . your nature."

The four of us — the master, the other American, the interpreter, and I — sat on floor cushions around the low table. In a few seconds I saw the wife of the master for the first time. A thin, smiling woman dressed in a kimono. She looked tired; I later discovered she had been ill. Up to now we had been shielded from the crisis: she cooked for the school and there was a question whether she was well enough to do this. She did manage it for the five days with the help of young women brought in from the outside. She carried four round, black lacquered, covered dishes on a tray. The meal was cold; it had been bought in the nearby suburban town.

My Western roommate and I followed our host's movements and took the cover off the dish. Uncovered was a neatly arranged array of rolled raw fish, rice, and seaweed; the impression was of a tight bouquet of flowers, a nosegay.

We ate slowly with our chopsticks during a slow-paced conversation about trivial things. Although I think of myself as capable of eating anything, I could not get very far with the raw fish. I have eaten raw fish before but it was always of room temperature; this was ice cold. I tried to eat as much as possible but could finish only about a third of the large dish. The master's wife removed our dishes and brought hot tea.

The evening was drawing to a close. The young lady helped the master's wife remove the dishes and arose to go. It was about 9:00 P.M. and dark; I asked her if she would like me to walk home with her. Since we were not yet in training, I assumed I would be permitted to leave the house.

"I live very near," she said, "I'm perfectly safe."

In a burst of Western politeness, I insisted. She said she would ask the master. I did not know until later that his agreement to my walking home with her was reluctantly given.

We put on our shoes at the door. This would be my last time out of the house for five days. We went out into the dimly lit, unpaved streets. A dog barked here and there. A light rain had begun to fall. The small street lights appeared vaguely through the mist and I could barely make out the small, seemingly paper thin houses which lined the streets. We crossed the railroad tracks and after walking another block we were at her house.

The young lady told me that she had only recently discovered that in her neighborhood was a Zen priest and she had come a week or so ago to inquire about Zen instruction. The master had offered her the five-day course and had asked her to interpret for the Westerners. Since college was in session and she was teaching, she could come only in the evenings. His invitation stood nonetheless; she would meditate when she could find time. He was not rigid about visitors or schedules, although most students come for the five days and follow all regulations.

I thanked her for her help in speaking with the master, we bowed, and I walked back slowly in the rain, thinking over what had occurred. What am I in for? I remember asking myself again.

CHAPTER III

B ACK IN THE HOUSE, off with my shoes, on with slippers, a walk through the small main room, a bow to the master who sat reading, off with the slippers, in my stockinged feet, into the bedroom. My roommate was looking through his bags, and I looked into mine for a toothbrush and toothpaste. Back to the door, on with the slippers, a walk through the main room, a bow to the master, through the hall to the newly added toilet room. Off with the soft slippers, on with wooden slippers, sliding the thin door open and then closed, into a tiny room with a small wash basin of porcelain. There was a small sliding, paned window. I opened it to see the view, but there was only an air vent. I brushed my teeth. Sliding another door, I found an even smaller room containing only a toilet. Finishing with the washroom, I slid the main door open again. Off with wooden slippers, on with soft slippers, walk through the main room, bow to the master, off with slippers, into the bedroom. These countless new details of living gradually became routine to me.

Time for bed. The master's wife showed us the closet in which bedding was stored and helped us make our beds on the floor. Some bed pads, a blanket folded pad size, a sheet to cover the blanket, and another blanket to cover me. A small face towel to cover the Japanese pillow, a small object much like a fully packed bean bag. I took off my clothes, covered myself with the blanket, and began my homework (the only bit of reading we were allowed to do). I propped myself up on my elbow, arranged the booklet so that I could see by the overhead, shaded electric light in the center of the room, and opened the pamphlet. This was the small booklet given to us earlier in the evening. Its contents were in Japanese and English.

How Zen Is Taught at the Zenrigaku-kai*

The meaning of Zen

Everyone wishes to be free of his inner pains. These pains arise because he feels or thinks of them — "I think, hence I am." If he neither feels nor thinks of anything at all, there is no pain. From morning to evening everyone lets his mind wander from one thing to another and feels different sensations. Thus, he presumes that the mind has to be used in the wandering state. Shakamuni Buddha (Gautama) succeeded in the method of using the mind in the immobile state — the way of Zazen (Zen meditations). By become-

---

* With Master Ishiguro's permission I have edited this pamphlet to make it easier for English-speaking people to read. I regret only that I have divested it of some of the charm of the original translation, but I believe my editing makes up in readability what it loses in charm.

ing free from his inner pains, he arrived at the Great Satisfaction.

The word, Zen, derived from Dhyana of Sanskrit, was translated in old Chinese as "Jo-ryo" which means to stop thinking various things one after another. Master Dogen (1200-1253), the founder of the Soto sect of Zen in Japan, said, "No-thinking is the right way of Zazen." Including Shakamuni Buddha, all great masters who have handed down the true tradition of Zen through the centuries have succeeded in this method.

The findings of Shakamuni Buddha

The first finding is as follows. The fundamental state of the water's surface is its flat state, which takes place when all conditions that cause waves disappear. The air, too, attains its fundamental state when no vibrations exist in it. Thus, the fundamental state of the mind may be considered to be its no-thinking state. This state is where nothing is thought — the unconditional state for which "I do not think, hence neither I nor they are" holds. Here the unconditionality implies a property possessed by the mind as well as by the water, the air, and so on. The mind returns to its fundamental state when there are no conditions. It makes changes unconditionally according to given causes. This is what is called Bussho or the Nature of Buddha.

The second is the finding of the conditionality of

the relation between causes and results. Take, for example, water or air. They do not show changes which are not derived from given causes. Shakamuni Buddha found that everything in the world has the property that it changes its state according to the law of causality, and named this Hossho, or the Nature or Law. Bussho, the unconditionality, will be clearly recognized when one experiences the method of using the mind in the immobile state; at the same time he will understand that Hossho, the conditionality, never fails to work at any instant where states of various things change.

The third is the finding of the never-failing union or cooperation of the conditionality and the unconditionality, despite their being opposite in character. This unity can neither be felt nor known. But this world is nothing but this unity, at any time and anywhere. Everything comes from this unity and disappears into it. Appearance and disappearance, both are due to the action of Bussho and Hossho, the properties of this unity. Every state of everything is thus a concrete representation of these two natures. That Bussho and Hossho are united into one is called Ittai-Sambo or Three Treasures. Every happening in either the natural world or the human society is due to Ittai-Sambo, in its appearance, disappearance and mutations.

When a man understands clearly the mechanism of Ittai-Sambo that prevails in the Universe, he will be unable to dare do things which entail evil results.

Neither will he be able to avoid doing things which entail good results and doing his best to help his fellow men.

In these realizations Shakamuni Buddha became the Buddha. The important aims of Buddha's teachings were to tell people these things. In this way all people can improve.

How a person may become free of inner pains

It is easy to see that one can hardly arrive at the great satisfaction by the method of using the mind in the wandering state. For comparison, let us take the case of a patient suffering from seasickness aboard a boat being rocked by waves. He cannot recover as long as he is aboard even if he is taught by others that the seasickness will be gone when he lands. The same is true for a man who sticks to the method of using the mind in the wandering state. He cannot become free from inner pains no matter how well he learns that the great satisfaction can be arrived at when he succeeds in the method of using the mind in the immobile state. When the patient lands on the pier the sickness will be over. Similarly, inner pains will disappear and all thoughts will be lost only when he succeeds in this method.

Therefore anyone who wishes to have the great satisfaction is obliged to experience the success in the method of using the mind in the immobile state. Then, just as Shakamuni Buddha had his first experience, so will any man realize that he has actually been free from inner pains. He will then feel the great satisfaction.

As stated before, this can be done by not thinking various things one after another.

On the traditional way of teaching Zazen

The traditional methods of teaching Zazen have been too precise in manners and forms, caring less about inner problems. Of course they taught students to be in "Munen-Muso" (no thoughts and no feelings), in another case to be in "Moo" (Nothing), or just to sit quietly, or to be in Koanzammai (absorbed in Zen questions). But these ways of teaching were something like forcing a person to jump from the ground to the top of the stairs. Many students must have tried in vain to arrive at the great satisfaction, asking themselves what results they had obtained after these long years of study.

On the method of teaching at the school of Master Horyu Ishiguro

Master Ishiguro entered into Zen some fifty years ago. He studied for a long time with Master Sogaku Harada of the Soto Sect. After having been given the final permit, Master Ishiguro began to teach students, using at first the traditional method. But he wished to improve the method in order to help people save themselves from inner pain as quickly and surely as possible. From January 1957 he began to apply his new method of teaching.

The first step of his method is to help the student

realize the value of Zen and understand its principles. The student is then given the first practice of using the mind in the immobile state. After he succeeds in this, the student is given the next one. Thus, one step after another, he is able to climb upstairs where he will find the great satisfaction. Anyone who wishes to become free from inner pains and arrive at the great satisfaction has the ability to do so.

I did not think much about what I had read. Some of the statements in the pamphlet had been made in one way or another by the master earlier in the evening. I had followed him, had understood or had a feeling for what he seemed to be saying. As I have said, I had read some Zen literature. Again, I do not believe I anticipated any great satisfaction from the five days; I do not recall even taking note of the words. The parts which made no sense to me I simply overlooked. Besides, I was exhausted from this day and the two days preceding.

I looked over at my roommate who was in his floor bed across the room. He had just finished reading and I asked if I could turn out the light. Lying and thinking about the evening, I drifted off and was awakened by my roommate's snoring. I listened for a few minutes and then awakened him by calling his name. The snoring stopped.

I remember the train passing, the whistle, the house shaking. I thought I would never go back to sleep. I also remember rising on my elbow to look out of the glass door, but it was dark and I could not see clearly. In a couple of minutes I was fast asleep.

CHAPTER IV

IT WAS 5:30 A.M. of the first day.

My roommate and I got up, took our turns shaving in our washroom and returned to our bedroom. One set of sliding doors at the side of our room had been opened to the small narrow dining room. As on our porch, one entire long wall was made of glass sliding doors. The table was long and low. Cushions were placed on the floor for sitting at the table. We were about to be introduced to the endless pleasures and rituals of taking meals in a Japanese household, something I had never done before.

The other students began to arrive — our first look at the people who would be sharing this experience. There were four men besides my roommate and me; three of the four appeared to be quite young, perhaps sixteen to eighteen years old. They were dressed in Western style — shirt and trousers. From what part of the house had they come, I wondered. Had they slept here? As they came in, they bowed as I did and we quietly and rather shyly gave our names. "San" is added to one's surname as an address; I became accustomed to answering to "Hubersan." I suppose it was at that breakfast that I took up the practice of calling the master "Roshi" as I heard the Japanese call him.

The term simply means master, and of course implies considerable respect.

We stood beside our cushions, placed our hands before us in prayer fashion; the Roshi said a prayer in Japanese, shook a small brass bell, and then we sat down.

Silence was protocol, although this was not rigid. In one kind of language or another we asked each other to pass food; we thanked each other. We seldom if ever talked any more than that. For the first few meals my roommate spoke a great deal as Westerners are apt to do at meals, but no one replied to him with more than polite, monosyllabic words. Actually there was no way of knowing if any of the other students understood him. Finally he fell silent.

The kinds of food served at breakfast were the same as those of every other meal. There was a small salad in a dish by itself; it had one small piece each of about five vegetables, most of which were unfamiliar to me. Soup was served in our individual lacquer bowls from a large cauldron placed on the table by the okusan (wife). Next to this cauldron was another filled with steaming rice cooked wet as the Japanese do. As I remember, stewed meat was served regularly. We had tea at every meal.

I found I longed for some variation at breakfast. Asked repeatedly if we wished any variation in the meals, my roommate and I finally asked if we might have eggs at breakfast, and on the second day we found them at our plate, along with toast, butter, and jam. Even a container of instant coffee and hot water.

Everyone waited until the last person had finished eating and then one of us poured tea into each person's soup and rice bowls. The custom is to save the slice of hard yellow vegetable from the individual salad and use it as a kind of dish brush. It is dropped into the bowls and moved around the inside surface with chopsticks. The function is to clean the bowls. The tea, with its flavoring of bits of food, is drunk at the end of the meal. I never became accustomed to drinking this unusual mixture, but I assumed manners did not require it of me. I found a bowl was provided for those who chose not to drink it. I looked about me for some sign of what to do next. The bowls were dried with one of two napkins provided for each of us, the bowls were laid one into the other, the first napkin folded and placed in the top bowl, the bowls then wrapped in the other napkin, tied at the top, and chopsticks carefully placed in their paper envelopes were put under the knot. I never tired of this practical, useful ritual.

We arose, placed our hands in prayer fashion; the Roshi said a prayer in Japanese, tapped a bell; and we left the table.

The Roshi came to my roommate and me and indicated that we were to sleep for an hour. I had discovered that my roommate suffered from a chronic back ailment, and this morning I began the practice of making both our beds. I removed the bedding from the porch closet where it was stored after each sleeping period, and arranged the blankets, sheets and bean bag pillows on the floor. I had no trouble sleeping.

One hour later one of the students came to our bedroom and led us through the central room and to the door where the Japanese boy had sat the night before. Just inside the door was a staircase. Climbing the stairs, we came to the only room on the second floor. This was the meditation room. I realized it served the added purpose of sleeping room for the Japanese students. As I walked in, one of the Japanese men was rolling up his bedding from the floor.

The room was long and narrow and the floor was covered with tatami. An oriental rug covered a large part of the tatami. At one end was a clear glass wall, a part of which slid open to a balcony. At the other end, standing as a kind of room divider, was an unpretentious altar structure with curtains draped from the ceiling, a Buddha figure in the center, some metal lotus flowers, a large metal lantern, and a small vase filled with fresh flowers. These were the only decorations in the room. The glass wall provided a soft brightness to the room and the white walls made the room seem very fresh. Behind the altar was storage room for the students' clothing and to the left was a small washroom.

The Roshi helped the students take their positions for meditation. Each person seated himself facing a side wall; half of the men were on one side of the room, the other half on the other side. The walls provoked no distraction; they were blank. The Roshi helped me get comfortable sitting on the floor. Two cushions were placed one on top of the other to raise my buttocks from the floor; my legs were crossed and my knees rested on the floor. My neck and back were completely straight. My back never became tired.

The Roshi arranged my hands very carefully. They

were put in my lap, right fingers together and closed over
the left, thumbnails touching and upright so that the nails
were on top. The thumbs stayed in the prescribed position
only if one were awake. As one dozed, they fell.

My eyes closed (I never mastered keeping my lids
slightly open as is apparently the very advanced way), I
began my meditation. The system had been described the
night before and I had memorized the sounds I was to
make and fix my mind on. We were to count in Japanese
to three by breaking up the syllables of each number in this
fashion:

$$HI\text{-}TO\text{-}TSU - U - U - U$$
$$HU\text{-}TO\text{-}TSU - U - U - U$$
$$MI\text{-}IT\text{-}TSU - U - U - U$$

The U was given an *oo* sound. There was nothing magic
about Japanese numbers; we could have counted in any
language, the numbers of which broke well into syllables.
Each number was said in a normal breath and rhythmi-
cally, the U's continuing until the breath expired. A normal intake of air and then the number 2 (HU-TO-TSU),
and then 3. After this, we were to return to the first number. The sound was to be in the throat, audible to oneself
but inaudible to others.

Subsequent exercises were audible to everyone if one listened, but it was important at first that the room was as
quiet as possible to aid in fixing the mind in the early
stages.

Again with the minimum of English, the Roshi ex-

plained that we were to *listen* to the sound we were making in our throats — and we were to listen to nothing else.

I began my meditation. I listened to HI-TO-TSU-U-U,
took a breath, and began to wonder what the function
of counting was. I returned to listening and then began to
think about why I was here. Back to counting and listening. And then more thoughts. What were other people
doing? Were they having as difficult a time of it? Had I
tipped the taxi driver sufficiently? Did the Roshi really
know what he was doing? Could I stand going through
this? My god, it was boring. My thumbs relaxed. I was
falling off to sleep. MI-IT-TSU-U-U. Should that sound
have been longer? No, that was a normal breath. Was I
breathing the right way? Would the train continue to pass
all day with its whistle and forceful shaking of the house?
Did I only imagine the house shook? Back to counting
and listening. HU-TO-TSU-U-U. MI-IT-TSU-U-U. I
could not possibly keep my mind on it.

Bored, irritated, exhausted, I was interrupted by the
sound of a bell in the room. I turned my head and discovered the Roshi; he held the bell and motioned for us to rise.
Following him, we walked slowly in a circle, one behind
the other, around the room. I guessed this was interjected
to allow us to stretch and to allow some relief from an impossible task. About four times around the room, another
tapping of the bell, and we sat down again.

I had perhaps never been so frustrated in my life. I tried
to continue the counting and listening but I did no better
with it. Again the frustration was interrupted by a bell. It
was 11:30. We had been in the room over two hours now.

We were to go downstairs one at a time for our private interview with the Roshi. Since the Roshi was already downstairs, I could have waited my turn by walking about the room or going out on to the balcony where there was a view over the rooftops of the suburb. With relief in sight, I decided to continue trying with my counting and listening until I was to go downstairs.

The private interview (dokusan) was held in our bedroom which, of course, was free of furniture except the low, round table. I had no idea about the ritual of the dokusan or what was to happen. We did not have any order of going in to see the Roshi; we went in according to who went downstairs first. I wondered how I could have a private interview when we did not speak the same language, and the interpreter was not to be here during the day.

I took off my slippers and walked into the bedroom. The Roshi was sitting on the floor in Japanese fashion, on his knees. I stood wondering what to do. He indicated that I should bow, go to my knees and bow again, this time all the way to the floor. As usual his instructions were given with gestures and the few English words he knew. I realized this was a definite ritual; I assumed it was a Buddhist ritual of respect for one's teacher. I recall being somewhat amused by the deep bowing, but I suppressed a smile. Oddly, I had the feeling that he was smiling but I did not know him well enough to be sure. I did not yet know that amusement might be shown about anything.

Having finished my bows, I sat upright again on my knees and looked at him. He looked at me for some time, seeming partly to try to read in my face what my reactions were and partly to be searching for English words.

With pencil in hand and tablet before him, he asked simply, "What per cent?" He pronounced it *par* cent and I never ceased in the next few days to find it amusing.

Somehow I knew that he was asking what per cent of time I was centered on the exercise. "Two," I replied. I was somewhat hesitant; I suppose I was waiting for criticism. He made a single mark in his tablet (I assume it was the number 2) and then looked up at me. He hesitated; he was searching for English words.

"Ah . . . you . . . try . . . try hard." He thought a second, nodded his head as if he were satisfied that he had said what he intended to say, and then smiled. He bowed his head; the dokusan was over.

Again he instructed me about the ritual. I bowed, got to my feet, bowed again, and backed my way to the door. The subsequent interviews followed the same ritual.

I returned to the room upstairs, seated myself on the floor, and continued my attempts to fix my mind on the counting. At about this time I began to notice severe pain in my knees — periodic sharpness and continuous burning, undoubtedly the result of having my knees bent for such long periods. I was distracted by it — only one of a thousand distractions, but a strong one. I would interrupt my attempts at centering my mind to rub my knees. I had no idea that the Roshi was observing me.

How painful will my knees become? Rubbing. HU-TO-TSU-U-U. Listening. What does the per cent have to do with it? What time is it? MI-IT-TSU-U-U-U. Listening. I'm sleepy. Counting. Not listening. I must really try to concentrate. Counting, listening. Counting, listening. I'm doing better at it. That is, of course, a distraction in itself. Counting, listening. Counting, listening. I nodded and pulled myself up with a start. I had fallen asleep.

I thought lunch would never come. Finally a metal gong was rung downstairs and all of us looked around. The Roshi was gone. We stretched, glanced at each other, smiled, arose, and went downstairs.

Lunch was taken with the same customs as breakfast. After lunch I again slept soundly for an hour and returned upstairs to my attempts at meditation. The afternoon went a little better, although my knees continued to hurt. When the afternoon dokusan came, I was able to estimate to the Roshi that I had been fixed on my listening about 10 per cent of the time.

The remainder of the afternoon was filled with feelings of anger, interest, frustration, determination, amusement — and what seemed to me to be a great deal of dozing.

Sometime during the afternoon I heard the Roshi talking to my roommate who sat behind me facing the opposite wall. When we got up to relax I saw that he had taken to sitting in a chair.

The Japanese students began to include me in their glances about the room. Occasionally one of them would smile. At one point I risked a shake of the head at the young man sitting next to me, and said, "Hard!" He grinned and said, "Yes."

When I became unusually frustrated or bored, I was

encouraged by the fact that other people around me were trying.

Finally dinner was announced. After dinner we again slept for an hour. I was becoming accustomed to the naps. I never had trouble going directly to sleep.

When I got up from my nap and passed through the main room, I met the young Japanese woman.

"How is the Zazen?" she asked.

I found that I did not want to talk and I answered briefly that it was hard. She came upstairs with the group, and I saw the Roshi instructing her in Zazen.

The evening went a little better but I was still having trouble with my knees and a thousand distracting thoughts.

Zazen over, we went downstairs and the Roshi spoke to the interpreter, my roommate, and me. This happened periodically; I assumed he was giving us part of what he gave the Japanese students at another time. During these infrequent and short conversations he spoke about Zen.

To his statements I could give only highly personal associations, but I was never asked to state them. Even if we could have communicated in a common language, I do not believe he would have pursued my associations to help me analyze them. This was left for me to do as I chose. He and I were in no way "in this thing together," as therapist and patient are apt to be. We were mutually sharing neither a review of my daily activities and thoughts nor a recounting of my past. He pointed to vague goals the content of which I would have to fill in for myself. He instructed me in meditation; he contributed to my comfort and the elimination of distraction. The rest was up to me.

The interpreter got up to go and I asked if she would like me to walk home with her. She seemed pleased but doubtful. She turned to the Roshi in a casual way, spoke, turned back to me, and smiled.

"You are not to leave the house." She seemed to expect his reply; I should have known he would try to prevent any distraction for me.

When she left, I returned to my room. As I took out our bedding from the porch closet, my roommate began to talk about Zazen — Did I see its similarity to one psychological principle or another? How was I doing? What did I think the function of counting was?

I was sure the rule against unnecessary conversation was crucial to the training and I wanted to follow the rules. I answered his questions perfunctorily, irritated. This occurred a few more times in the next day or two until I mustered the courage to tell him that I did not want to break the rule against unnecessary conversation. I gradually ignored his overtures to conversation and he became more silent. Perhaps there is something important about this. Before he became almost completely silent, my irritation reached a high point. I recall thinking I would push myself to follow all the rules despite distractions provided by my roommate. He was unquestionably a goad, perhaps an important one.

I turned off the light and got into my bed on the floor.

"The hardest work I have ever done," I remember thinking as I fell off to sleep.

CHAPTER V

THE SECOND MORNING of Zazen went much the same as the previous afternoon. I dozed a great deal, partly, I believe, because I was still tired from my long trip to Japan, and partly because I was bored, frustrated, and discouraged. My knees continued to hurt.

I was trying hard to attend to my counting and listening when suddenly I felt a tap on the shoulder. I was startled and I turned to find the Roshi beside me. Again he looked at me in an apparent effort to find English words.

"Floor . . . for Japanese. No Westerner." It must have been apparent to him that I was determined to learn to sit on the floor, but he made the decision for me that the distraction was too great. He motioned for me to get up. He went to a closet and brought back a chair on which he placed a cushion; he also put a cushion on the floor for my feet. He indicated that I should sit on the chair. I again sat very straight; my back was supported by the chair. He put my feet on the cushion. My hands were in the usual position, thumbnails up to check my dozing. He stayed beside me until he was satisfied that I was comfortable. My knees stopped hurting immediately.

I began to do a little better at listening to my counting

and cutting away other thoughts. Despite the dozing, I was able to report a somewhat higher *par* cent of time in attending to my counting and listening.

After lunch and the usual nap we returned to the room upstairs. This time as we seated ourselves and were about to begin counting, the Roshi interrupted. He announced that we had finished the first phase of our training. He again spoke in Japanese and then would attempt an English word or two of translation. Gradually and hesitatingly the young man who sat next to me began to translate. He seemed to feel totally inadequate to the task, but there was a task to be done and he did it. Actually his English was quite fluent; the Roshi had obviously not been aware of this.

The Roshi explained that we were to produce a single syllable — MU (the U, as usual, being an *oo* sound) — in a rhythmic fashion. On each expulsion of breath we were to produce MU-U-U-U until the air was out. Again it was to be throaty and barely audible. Mu (or Moo), I realized later in rereading the Roshi's pamphlet, means "nothing."

I welcomed the variation. It later occurred to me that repetition produces boredom, and boredom brings distraction. I assume the Roshi uses variation to cut down the time required to produce complete centering of attention. I must add that I *think* this was a planned part of his method; I had neither opportunity nor language to discuss his methods with him. Furthermore I did not want to intellectualize at the moment.

My dozing was becoming less frequent. I was clearly

doing better and by the time the afternoon dokusan came, I was able to report a still higher per cent of attention.

Sometime in the afternoon I had two peculiar sensations. I do not know how long either of them lasted. I first noted a feeling that my body was becoming heavier and heavier. The feeling finally disappeared. Later in the afternoon I had the feeling that my body was growing larger and larger, almost as if it were filling the room. I had experienced the latter feeling only at one other time in my life; I recall that during childhood it occurred on several occasions before sleep.

Much later in the afternoon I had a striking insight. In the middle of my sound-listening periods I realized that no matter what thought or feeling I had, it passed on. It either never recurred or never recurred in quite the same way. I realized that nothing will ever come again as it comes to me at any one moment. Nothing exists but what exists now.

Later I recognized this as one of the cardinal Buddhist principles — the impermanence of all things, the constancy of change.

These were not totally new thoughts to me, but in the intensity of observation of what went through my mind I experienced the idea as I never had before. At each moment only sound, then only listening, then breathing, then sound, then listening. Then distraction — a face, a thought, a feeling, an idea. Anger, frustration. Would the distraction last? That was the question. Will it last? And then it struck me. Will what last? Was this not the ques-

tion I was always asking myself? Will this pleasure last?
This anxiety? What can I do to make it go away? Always
the avoidance of what is going on at the present moment.
Always the concern about the future, tomorrow, next year,
the next moment. What next moment?

Oddly my reaction to the ringing of the bell, this time
the dinner bell, had changed; I was not quite as relieved as
I had been previously. I was pleased to stop, but the eager-
ness to stop Zazen was no longer there.

I believe it was that afternoon when my roommate
began leaving the house. When I came downstairs to eat, I
found him cleanly shaven with the smooth, shaved look
that only a barber produces. He explained that he had had
to have a real shave and had gone into the neighboring village. During the following days he continued to visit the
village during Zazen and would usually bring back candy
or ice cream for all of us. In the middle of Zazen I would
hear soft moving, would look up, and see him tiptoeing out
of the room. I never knew how much time he spent away
from the center.

I was becoming quieter. I was generally less distracted,
more centered on what I was doing at any one moment.

After dinner and sleep the interpreter again came to sit
in Zazen with us. When the evening session was over, I
spoke briefly with her. These brief conversations allowed
by the Roshi were, I believe, intended as an opportunity
for us to ask the interpreter anything we wished since his
own lack of English did not allow him fully to know what
was on our minds.

When she came up to me, she was obviously troubled.

"You're changed," she said. "You look different."

I had no reply to this and did not really want to think about it. I was not willing to attend to framing a reply. I knew also that the minute I began explaining or labeling, my attention would shift to the explanation and away from the quiet centering of attention.

There was no suggestion of my walking home with her; the Roshi had made that quite clear to both of us the previous evening.

Quietly I went to bed. The interpreter was right. I was different. I suppose the word is undistracted. I was centered on what I was doing, although I did not think of that at the time. As I looked back on it, I was neither happy nor unhappy; I had dropped even that kind of labeling.

I now seldom paid attention to the train or its whistle. At those times when I did notice it, I listened to it. No longer concerned about its distracting me, I quite enjoyed it when I heard it.

CHAPTER VI

THE MORNING OF THE THIRD DAY we continued with the same exercise. Lunch was quiet, and then the nap came. In the afternoon the Roshi gave us a new exercise, our third. We were to make a single sound with no rhythm or pulsations. The sound was the previous one, MU. It was to be made with power. As demonstrated for us, the U part of the sound was almost like a GR-R or growl. We were no longer to hold in the sound; it was to be audible. It seemed simply like another exercise to me; not until later that evening did I realize the quality of strength and power and even the strangeness of it to an observer.

I realized now that each of the exercises required considerable attention even to do them accurately. The strong MU sound captured my attention and interest. One could hardly make the sound strongly without devoting attention to it. Actually this was true of all the exercises. At first I was somewhat distracted by the loud noise of the five of us making the strong MU sound. The distractions, however, soon disappeared when I began making the sound as prescribed and listening to it. When I went for the afternoon dokusan my *par* cent had risen to an estimate of about 50 per cent of the time centered on the task.

By this time I was no longer thinking about whether or not I was doing well. I had stopped making comparisons of this kind; I had become free from that kind of distraction.

Dinner and nap came and went. I returned to the upstairs room and noted in passing through the door that our interpreter was speaking softly to the Roshi. Totally involved with Zazen by this time, I did nothing but note the fact that she was there.

The last bell was rung and I went downstairs. There in the central room was our interpreter; she walked toward me immediately as I entered the room. She was distraught.

"Please forgive me," she said, "I'm completely shaken. I've never seen anything like that — to come into a room and see all of you doing that. I just can't take it. I don't think I can stay. I feel terrible about leaving you both this way, but I don't think I shall be able to come back. Please forgive me."

My first reaction was anger. I needed her to translate in the dokusan. I wondered if I would have to stop Zazen. I had forgotten that my Zazen neighbor could speak some English; he seemed so shy that I did not think of him as an interpreter. I could do nothing about convincing her to stay. I said simply that she must not worry about us. She left seemingly undecided about returning. The Roshi seemed undisturbed by the incident.

That was the end of the third day. I knew I would continue with or without her interpreting.

CHAPTER VII

THE ROUTINES — eating, dokusan, naps — continued as I have described them. My relationship with the group had changed, however. At first I had felt very much an outsider, a Western curiosity; now I felt I was a part of the group. In particular, the boy sitting next to me in Zazen became friendly. I would occasionally have to ask him for a clarification of the Roshi's instructions; he seemed always to want to help me. I was impressed by his unwavering attention to the exercises; his presence more than any of the others' often encouraged me when I felt like resting.

Sometime during the fourth day a new person came. At one point I looked up and saw a man of about twenty-five sitting on the floor near the balcony, a short distance from the rest of us. He sat in full lotus position, legs crossed and upturned feet resting on the opposite thighs. I remember thinking he must be a former student because of the lotus posture; it is a difficult position to assume and to maintain. He never talked to anyone. I did not know then that his presence would be crucial to me the next day.

I thought no more about the interpreter. It never again crossed my mind that I might have to quit for any reason.

Early that day, the fourth day, the Roshi gave us a totally new exercise. Holding a piece of paper and a pen in his hands, the Roshi called us together to sit near him. He drew a simple picture of a short funnel with a long beak. He explained that we were to produce a prolonged MU sound (the beak) and then gradually increase the force of the sound (the funnel) to a crescendo. The beak part was to be about two-thirds of an exhalation; the funnel the remaining one-third. During the latter one-third the face, shoulder, and arm muscles were to be strongly tensed. The increase in volume was to be steady, not wobbly or varying up and down. We were instructed to listen to the prolonged MU but *not* to the last one-third. Our hands were to shift position drastically; each was made into a fist and placed on the thigh.

While I listened to the description intently and seriously, I found it amusing. It was ludicrously ferocious. I smiled openly. I was beginning to learn that there was nothing so sacred or serious that I could not express my amusement about it.

We followed the exercise all day. I do not remember hearing the train at all. I was occasionally aware of the loud sounds made by the other students around me, but this awareness was momentary. Moments of my life, thoughts, faces, uncomplicated sexual images devoid of fantasy or story quality came briefly and went.

During the morning I felt another peculiar bodily sensation. My body seemed to rise, while the floor, which I could not see since my eyes were closed, was sinking. I have no idea how long or how often I felt this. The feeling was, I recall, neither frightening, pleasant, nor unpleasant; it simply occurred and I observed it.

The afternoon session was without incident. I reported in my dokusan that I was focused about 80 percent of the time.

That evening the interpreter returned. She had apparently thought over the situation and had resolved her conflict. I was pleased. I liked her and needed her assistance; my attention to the exercises had reached a point where I wanted an easy exchange in the dokusan with no language barriers.

The interpreter and I went in to see the Roshi when my turn came. She sat on the floor in Japanese fashion with her legs behind her; she placed herself to the side where she was unobtrusive. When she was there to translate, the Roshi could express himself fully; he did not have to look for English words as he did when he and I were alone.

I faced the Roshi. As always, he looked directly at me.

"What did you hear during the last one-third of the exercise?" he asked.

"Nothing," I replied.

"What did you feel?"

"Strength," I found myself replying. I had not thought of the word before he asked me.

And then he said, "That is your nature. That has always been there to come out."

This was the dokusan as I remember it.

CHAPTER VIII

IT WAS THE FIFTH DAY. I took no particular cognizance of the fact. Looking back on it, I was eating more slowly; my movements were slower. What I did not choose to give my attention to (the train and its whistle, the loud noises of the current Zazen exercise) I was unaware of. What I chose to attend to (Zazen, meals, gestures, brushing my teeth, the thoughts and images passing through my mind) I was acutely aware of.

I arose from bed, washed and shaved, practiced Zazen, and came to breakfast. There the Master made an announcement. I find it among my papers, written in the handwriting of my Zazen neighbor, the serious boy. I must have asked him to do this but I do not recall the circumstances.

The translation was this: "The last practice of today's Zazen is just equal to this four days' practice. It is just for this last Zazen that we have held this Zen gathering or 'sesshin' for these five days. You must not neglect this last chance. Please do your best and increase your efforts."

In this announcement the Roshi did not say *why* one should do his best or increase his efforts. He did not say what the last chance was for. I believe my only goal at the time was to center my attention as I had been instructed. It was my last chance to do just that.

After the usual morning nap, we went upstairs. Seated again, we were given the fifth exercise, a variation of the previous one. This time the beak of the funnel, the steady MU sound, was to be short and was to be followed by a longer U of intensity rising to a crescendo. The ending of the sound was to be cut off sharply. We were to listen to it all.

The time must have been eight o'clock.

For some time there was little variation in my previous high degree of centering my mind. The new exercise involved no great variation, although there was the longer intense sound and muscular tension, the sharp ending and total listening.

Gradually I must have become completely focused on the exercise. I do not think that anything else went through my mind.

And then — it was late in the morning — a white, clear screen came before my eyes. In front of the screen passed, or rather, floated, simple images — faces, objects. I have no clear recollection of the images. A rush of feeling came over me.

I burst into tears; the tears became quiet sobbing.

I do not remember at what point I had stopped the exercise.

I can state my feeling, but I am not sure I can communicate it with any real meaning. I would like not to be mysterious; I would like to communicate it clearly, at the same time knowing that it may be impossible.

My feeling was that I was seeing something of great importance, as if everything fitted together for the first time. What had all my life struggles been about? Things were very clear and very simple.

I do not know how long I sat sobbing. Someone was at my side. He had his hand on my shoulder. It was my Zazen neighbor, the boy who sat next to me. He took my arm and I arose from my chair; we walked slowly together down the stairs. The new member of our group, the quiet man who had come on the fourth day, was downstairs waiting for me. I realized he was to be my interpreter; he had apparently volunteered.

He and I entered the dokusan room. I bowed and sat on my knees facing the Roshi as usual; I was still sobbing. The quiet man sat to the side. He translated easily and fluently. As he translated he looked directly at me. He now seemed warm, interested, and to want me to understand clearly what was being said to me.

"You have seen kensho," the Roshi said simply. I was aware that kensho meant a glimpse into one's own nature.

I did not reply. There was a long pause. The Roshi said something in Japanese and pointed in front of him. I looked at the quiet man.

"He says to come close to him." On my knees I slid closer.

"No, closer." I slid forward. Our knees were almost touching.

He opened his mouth quickly and burst forth with a loud sound, like a sharp "Ah!" I started. He looked at me.

"What did you feel?" he asked.

"Surprise."

"And after that?"

"Nothing."

A pause. My ankles were hurting. I rubbed them.

"Are you feeling well?" he asked.

"Yes. Only my ankles hurt." I had not become accustomed to sitting on my turned-under feet in the Japanese way.

"Get up and walk about."

I arose and walked about, rotating my feet to move my aching ankles. Relieved, I returned to my sitting position.

The Roshi looked at the place where I had walked.

"Are you able to see the footsteps?" the Roshi asked.

"No."

He nodded his head. "They were not there before and are not there now. There was nothing in your life before and nothing in the future, only —" and he burst forth again with "Ah!" This time I did not start. I looked at him. There was a pause.

"What do you think of life and death?" he asked.

"I don't think about it," I answered honestly.

"There is no life and death, no me, no you, only —" and he almost shook the room with "Ah!"

Again he looked at me intently for a few seconds and said, "Now you must rest. No more Zazen. Go up the stairs and sit quietly."

I bowed to him and to the quiet man and arose. My crying had stopped. I returned upstairs and sat quietly in my usual place until lunch. I was aware of the sounds around me. People continued with Zazen, the train passed and whistled, occasionally feet moved across the room. I listened, thoughts and faces and ideas passed through my mind, and I looked and listened.

Lunch was silent. I slept for an hour and returned to the room upstairs. I sat quietly again. The afternoon dokusan hour came. I waited my turn and went downstairs. Again the quiet man was with me. I entered the room, bowed, and smiled at the Roshi. He returned my smile and then looked serious.

"You have succeeded in Zen," he said.

I did not reply.

"Did you come here with serious personal problems?" he asked.

"No." He looked at me, paused a few seconds, and nodded.

"You must continue Zazen or this will become only a distantly remembered experience. I know you are busy in the big city. But in your busy life, sit in Zazen each day if only for five minutes. Begin with the third stage. But do not begin until one hour after eating. Otherwise, it will be bad for your stomach. Do not do the exercise from the stomach, but from below the navel — as if you were pushing the navel up."

I nodded.

"And remember. Do only that which is right — for a time and a place and a situation. Reject any action that has not these three conditions. And do good things for your fellow men."

He again looked intently at me for a few seconds and nodded. And then he smiled.

I smiled, bowed, arose . . . and forgetting the ritual, turned around and walked to the door. Still smiling, I turned back to him and bowed. Smiling, he deeply nodded his head.

The remainder of the afternoon I sat quietly in my chair. No one suggested I do anything else, and I wanted to sit quietly. Some of the people around me continued in Zazen. I did not observe who was there.

Dinner was silent. Again we returned to the upstairs room, and again I sat quietly. At an early hour a bell sounded from downstairs. The last Zazen was over.

We went to the dining room where all of us, including our interpreter, sat together for the last time. The Roshi's wife had prepared tea and Japanese cookies. My roommate had brought ice cream and candies from the neighboring village. I felt a festive air about the occasion; it was like a party.

Very little was said. We ate quietly. The Roshi praised the refreshments and thanked my roommate. The interpreter translated as usual.

And then something happened which changed the atmosphere.

My roommate looked at the Roshi and said, "I'd like to ask a question."

The interpreter translated. The Roshi looked up and nodded.

And then my roommate asked, "How many people succeeded?"

The interpreter, glancing at the Roshi as if he might

have understood, and then looking down, translated the question. The Roshi did not raise his eyes immediately. There was a pause. And then he looked around the group.

"Does anyone mind if we talk of this?" he said to the interpreter for her to translate.

The group was silent. I did not look up. The Roshi waited.

And then he said, "Two failed."

After a short silence I offered the Roshi an American cigarette and then offered cigarettes to the others; I had done this often. I was offered a Japanese cigarette. We sat quietly and smoked. From across the table, the serious boy asked for my address and I wrote it down as he wrote his. A few others did the same. When everyone had finished his cigarette, the Roshi indicated that we could arise, and people began to move in various directions to collect their belongings. I remembered the scores of times I had been through the end of school in Texas — the moving about, the packing, passing friends in the halls and smiling.

I went into the bedroom to pack. My roommate was not there. As I leaned over my luggage, I turned and saw the Roshi beside me. He said in his studied English, "You stay? Tonight here. You stay?" I was surprised. I smiled and nodded. I returned my bags to the corner of the room. As the Roshi left, my roommate came in. I helped him get his luggage. I stayed with him as he packed. He did not ask me why I was not preparing to go. I had been almost completely silent for at least four days and he had not been able to talk with anyone except the interpreter. We now had very little to say to each other. He did, however, make a parting statement.

"This is not the real Zen, of course," he said as he packed. He did not look up.

Not knowing what he really wanted to communicate, I had no reply.

"I don't really know," I said.

That was the end of it.

My Zazen neighbor, the serious boy, looked into the room and smiled. He had come to say goodbye. I left my roommate and walked through the door to the main room where the serious boy stood waiting. We shook hands and bowed. I thanked him for his help; he grinned. He asked me to write to him. I walked with him to the front hallway where he sat on the step and put on his shoes. He got up, lifted his few belongings which he had wrapped in a small bundle, and bowed to the Roshi and his wife who stood beside me. He opened the front door, looked around at us again, smiled and waved, and left.

People were leaving, one by one. I looked for the quiet man and found him in the main room. "Thank you," I said as I bowed. He smiled broadly; it was the first time I had seen him smile. We gave each other our addresses and planned to meet in Tokyo in the next few days.

My roommate came from the bedroom with his bags. Someone went to find him a taxi, and I carried his bags to the street. The Roshi, his wife, and I waved to him as the taxi moved off.

Finally only the interpreter was left. I asked her if I

might walk home with her. She turned to the Roshi who did not need a translation; he nodded.

She and I walked again through the suburban streets. How long had it been since I was outside? There was no mist; it was not raining. The street lights shone brightly on the houses. When we arrived at her house, she asked me to come in to meet her family. They were congregated in the living room when we came inside; I realized my visit had been planned. I sat for a few minutes, but I did not really want to be there at the moment, making conversation. I felt Zen would be a topic and eventually it came up. I turned it away, unable at the moment to communicate anything about my experience.

I returned to the Roshi's house and the okusan helped me prepare my bed.

I was alone for the first time in five days . . . was it only five days? I took off my clothes and lay down in my floor bed. I propped myself up on my elbow and looked out of the glass doors of the porch. The moon was shining and I could see the small trees outside. The train passed and looked alive with light; people sat in the coaches reading their newspapers. The whistle blew, the house shook, and I found myself smiling.

CHAPTER IX

THE NEXT MORNING I arose casually and washed and shaved. The three of us had breakfast; for the first time the Roshi's wife sat at the table. I had my eggs, toast made in the toaster, jam, butter, and instant coffee. When breakfast was over, I put my bowls and napkins together in the usual way as if I would be there to eat again. I helped the Roshi's wife clear the table. She would not let me help her clean the dishes.

Somehow or other the Roshi and I communicated quite easily. I spoke simply and slowly and the Roshi searched his limited vocabulary to tell me how he established the school, how he wished to come for a visit to the United States to instruct in Zazen, and other things I do not recall now. When spoken words were difficult to understand, we wrote them and sometimes even drew pictures to communicate what we wished to say to each other. The Roshi translated to his wife what we said.

After breakfast the Roshi went into my bedroom and sat on the floor by the low table. I followed him. I do not remember any special preparation for what followed. The Roshi's wife brought red and black inks, brushes, seals, and some heavy, picture-size, white cards with gold edges.

While she and I watched, the Roshi began painting calligraphy on the cards with his Japanese brush and black ink. He handed a card to me, obviously a gift. The only part of it I could read was my own name. I asked him to translate and I wrote as he attempted to translate with his limited vocabulary. What I wrote down was the following:

> Congratulations, J. T. Huber has seen unconditional nature.
> In nothing there is no end.
> There is flower and moon and high house. Many clouds in the sky.
> All people cool. [He explained that people in pain are "hot."] Moreover with effort comes high understanding.

He used two seals, pushed them one by one into a pad of red ink, and carefully made impressions on the card. One of the seals carried his own name. The other impressed the words, No moving mind.

I was amused by the congratulations. I bowed my head and thanked him.

The Roshi's wife brought out a painting she had done — a ferocious and amusing male face on a large sheet of fine rice paper; the size was appropriate for a scroll. This, too, was a gift for me.

The okusan put away the paints and the Roshi said we must take photographs. I indicated that I wanted to change clothes for the occasion. He seemed pleased, and the two of them went to collect the camera equipment. I changed from my usual casual clothes to my dark blue suit, white shirt, and tie.

When I arrived upstairs he first showed me a photograph of a young Frenchman and explained that he was the only other Westerner up to this point who had "succeeded in Zen" with the Roshi's training. The young man, he explained, had sat unsuccessfully for twenty-one five-day "sesshins" and on the twenty-second he had succeeded. The Roshi smiled broadly as he showed me the photograph.

We began to prepare to take photographs. We arranged and rearranged the pillows and chairs. All three of us sat on chairs beside each other in front of the Buddhist "altar." The Roshi quickly got up as if he had remembered something important, returned with the white card of congratulations he had prepared this morning, and placed it on my lap. He looked us over with obvious approval, smiled, then looked serious, went to arrange and set his camera, quickly returned to his chair. The camera clicked. He took two more pictures of us and we returned downstairs with the camera equipment.

I felt it was time to go.

I gathered my luggage, the usual half empty suitcase and fairly full zipper bag I always carried on long trips. I went to the porch for the last time. I slid the glass doors open and faced the garden. I do not remember if the train passed. Picking up my bags I went to the front door where the Roshi and his wife stood waiting. Off with my guest slippers, I sat down on the hall step and put on my own shoes. The Roshi indicated that he and the okusan would guide me to the street where I could find a taxi. We walked together in the sun along the narrow street. It was a bright day. Coming to a small intersection they stopped and the Roshi pointed to a parallel road, busy with traffic. This was where the taxis were.

I put my bags down, put my hands together in the usual position, and bowed. The Roshi and his wife did the same. When I raised my head, they both looked directly into my eyes. All three of us smiled. I lifted my bags and began walking away. I looked back every few yards. They bowed each time and smiled. When I reached the main road I looked back for the last time; they bowed and then waved. They walked slowly toward their home, looking back and waving until they were out of sight. I can still see them.

CHAPTER X

How can i tell the next part of the story? Perhaps we do not describe things well when we have lived them fully; could that odd twist be true? Perhaps all of us find it difficult to communicate our feelings when we are really feeling something deeply, when we are really seeing things clearly. How does one tell another person what it is like to be fully aware of what one is feeling, what it is like to love, to feel anger?

I returned to Tokyo and began sightseeing, going to restaurants, meeting people. Then a visit to Kyoto with its tiny, pebbled gardens, its small summer residence of the Emperor, its ancient Shogun's palace, its countless, huge temples.

I was seeing it all as if I had never seen it before. I seemed almost to have a new pair of eyes, new ears, new abilities to taste and smell and feel. I had learned to give my full attention to whatever I was doing at any one moment and I wondered if I had ever really done this before.

Gradually I began to see I was eating when I was hungry, not when it was "time to eat." I began to eat what I wanted to eat, not because it was placed before me, because others were eating, because we must have three good meals a day. I was reminded of the psychological study of small children who, allowed to eat what they wanted to eat, chose in the end a balanced diet. The extra weight I had picked up in my early forties began to disappear and has not reappeared. Perhaps we have no "weight problem" if we eat when we are hungry and eat what we really want to eat.

I began to feel I had never really tasted things before. I ate less, drank less, and enjoyed both experiences more. Even being with people became a new kind of experience to me. I had always been gregarious — and often undiscriminating. Now I chose *whom* I wanted to be with and now I was *with* them. I was seeing and choosing what I wanted to do — speak with someone, drink coffee, read a book.

I saw what I was doing as if I had never seen it before. And the pleasures I found in it all were something I could not have imagined.

I began to wonder if I should go on to Burma for more meditation. The changes which had come about in me were so new and so all encompassing that I wondered if I could closet myself, if I *wanted* to take myself away from the world to engage in more meditation so soon after my experiences with the Roshi.

Perhaps I should have asked the Roshi, but it had not occurred to me. Instead I wrote to the Burmese meditation center. I explained that I had been in meditation in Japan and I wondered if I should undertake more meditation so soon; it would be only one month later.

The Sayadaw replied immediately. His letter was short

and cordial. They were expecting me; I should come. I should let him know my exact time of arrival, airline and flight number.

I do not believe I gave it any more thought. I had only Shattock's book to give me any idea of what I would be getting into and that information was not enough. The entire trip had, after all, centered on my going to Burma. I would take the Sayadaw's advice and go. I did not ponder the decision as I might have previously. I had only very little information to use; I weighed it, made the decision, and thought no more about it.

From Japan I went to Hong Kong and then Kuala Lumpur and Penang in the Malayan States, and Bangkok. From Bangkok I took the plane to Rangoon, Burma. I had no way of knowing what was about to happen.

CHAPTER XI

I ARRIVED at the airport in Rangoon in the early evening of July 21. The view from the plane was of endless green; it was like a jungle. The airport was very modern as most of the airports of large cities throughout the world are today — modern and indistinguishable one from another.

Off the plane, I stepped into the passport line and waited; the line was moving slowly. I looked around for someone from the Meditation Center; I should see someone, maybe two or three people, with shaven heads and wearing saffron yellow robes. Instead I saw both men and women dressed in ankle-length cotton skirts, called longyis; the women wore blouses, the men shirts. It passed through my mind that the longyis must be very comfortable and cool. I supposed I would buy one eventually, perhaps tomorrow, and wear it in the Center. I did not want to stand out as a foreigner any more than necessary.

No, there was no one in a saffron robe. Perhaps they had not yet received my letter saying when I would arrive. Or perhaps no one could be spared to come for me. The Center was well known; I would simply get into a cab and ask to be taken there.

The line was hardly moving. Some American far ahead

of me in line was having difficulty with his passport, or was it a German? No, the passport was like mine.

I kept thinking about Bangkok. I had not really wanted to leave. Only this afternoon I had been there sightseeing, riding along the klongs in a small boat with Thai friends. Standing in line, I kept thinking about it and wondering if I could have enjoyed it as much if I had not been in meditation in Japan.

And now here I was in Rangoon ready to practice meditation again, all day every day for three weeks. I remember asking myself, Should I be here?

It was my turn in the passport line. The neatly uniformed immigration agent looked at my passport, glanced at me, looked at the passport again.

"I'm sorry, you don't seem to have a Burmese visa."

I could not quite believe what I heard him say. With assurance I took the passport from him and looked through it; I was certain he had overlooked the visa. My passport was very full, and I could not read all the entries in many languages. I searched through it, then both of us searched. No visa. My travel agent must have overlooked getting it for me.

The immigration man announced rather coolly that without a visa I could not stay in the country. I was perplexed and he must have seen it in my face. In no time at all three more immigration agents were with us watching the proceedings. I told the first man that I was expected by the Mahasi Sayadaw at the Meditation Center. He seemed surprised and asked me if I had some evidence of correspondence with the Sayadaw. He called someone to get my luggage and I scoured through it for a letter from the Sayadaw. I found the most recent letter and handed it to him. He read it slowly; the other three read over his shoulder. During the reading, one and then another of them glanced up at me. One would smile; another would slowly and sympathetically shake his head. The slight humor of the situation and their obvious warmth made me feel better. I felt I was on the way to being allowed to stay in the country. They seemed to be very impressed by the letter; the Sayadaw was, I gathered, a well-known and highly respected person. I had already heard that the previous prime minister had meditated regularly with the Sayadaw.

Not knowing enough about the new government, I had miscalculated. Impressed or not, the agent had made up his mind; he had no choice but to follow government regulations. But by now his face had softened.

"I'm very sorry," he said, "you can stay only seventy-two hours in the country. You must procure a visa either here or elsewhere." I had visions of returning to Bangkok and my friends. "You are not permitted to return to Bangkok, but you may go to your next destination to get a visa . . . or perhaps the Mahasi Sayadaw can help you."

I was incredulous and angry, but he had obviously made his final pronouncement. There was nothing further to say to him; I knew any further pleas would be ignored. I did not know how I would solve the problem, but for now I needed to get to town and start working on it. I did, after all, have seventy-two hours. I asked about transportation to the city and the immigration agents took me to the waiting airport bus.

I had the name of a small hotel used mostly by Burmese people, and in a short time I was there. The hotel part began on the second floor; on the first floor was an ice-cream parlor. The skirted desk clerk who sat at a writing desk in the combined registration office and dining room signed me in, and another skirted man took my bags to a third-floor room. The room was small; the only furniture was an iron bed, a chest of drawers, a table desk, and a wash basin. I immediately pulled the curtains aside and opened the windows. Before me was the main street of Rangoon. Rain was pouring down by now; it was the monsoon season. The sidewalks were lined with people in longyis holding umbrellas; they were waiting for the next performances at the numerous large and modern movie houses on both sides of the street. It was Saturday night. I was happy with the view.

I went downstairs, ordered a curry dinner, and phoned an American to whom I had a letter of introduction. He asked me to lunch the next day. I wanted him to invite me to his house that evening. I was lonely.

Next day a car was sent for me and I was taken to the American's house where I was greeted at the door by him and his Viennese psychologist wife. He had seemed cool over the telephone, but I discovered he was quiet and shy — and very helpful. The previous night I had told him that I did not have a visa; he had already invited an associate to come to help me. The associate, a former Burmese government official, came after a few minutes and stayed long enough to discuss the situation. Seeing the predicament I was in, he was determined to get a visa for me. I did not know at the time how interested he was in meditation.

For the next two days he drove me from place to place through the lush green countryside pleading for a visa. He took me to see the Mahasi Sayadaw briefly, but in the end even the Sayadaw could do nothing about it. My brief encounter with the Sayadaw gave me very little impression of him. The Burmese gentleman and I had walked in and sat on the floor for a few minutes while he spoke to the Sayadaw. The Sayadaw seemed concerned but quiet; I was told he would write a letter to the immigration authorities.

As we drove along in the chauffeured car, my Burmese acquaintance, a man in his sixties, spoke continuously about meditation. He was very impressed that I had come. He was a Buddhist and had always planned to meditate but had never done it. "Some day I shall do it," he said, and I had the feeling it was the most important consideration in his life.

"You Americans," he said, "you would meditate; you would have the strength, the vigor, the determination for it. How well you would do it. And what satisfaction you would derive from it. And what a difference it would make to the world."

Close to seventy-two hours of pleading and no visa. My helper apologized time and time again for his ineffectiveness but could do nothing more about it. "If we only had more time," he kept saying.

In preparation for the possibility of failure, I had made a plane reservation to Calcutta leaving just short of seventy-two hours after my arrival. It was an enormous extra expense but I had to have the visa. My helper took me to the airport, and I was off on a 600 mile flight for a visa. I knew a flight returned to Rangoon from Calcutta about an hour and a half after my arrival there, and I was determined to make it; I wanted no further delays. Arriving in Calcutta I quickly found a taxi, explained my goal, was driven at breakneck speed through the crowded streets and roads. I sat back and enjoyed the ever-changing view from the taxi windows — people everywhere, people dressed in loin-cloths, white linen suits, sarongs, any and everything; hundreds of small shops on the sidewalks displaying everything imaginable, bicycles everywhere, chickens and cows in the middle of the road. The driver never took his hand off the horn. It was a precarious and endless drive, and I was so interested I hardly thought about the visa.

After a half hour in the center of the town I had my visa and was back in the waiting cab. The plane was late in take-off and I made it. That same afternoon I was back in the Burmese meditation center sitting on the floor speaking with the Mahasi Sayadaw.

CHAPTER XII

I HAD TAKEN A TAXI from the airport to the Center. I took
my bags to the steps of the Sayadaw's house where I
found a saffron-robed priest whom I discovered later was
the assistant to the Sayadaw. He was short and rather
round. He was an intense man. I never really understood
him. In English he asked me to wait and said that he
would telephone the home of my interpreter who would
probably come immediately. I never discovered why the
assistant did not interpret for me, since his English was
very clear and fluent.

About a half hour later, my official interpreter arrived.
He was a man of about sixty, again a previous minister of
the government, now retired. He told me he came to the
Center for periodic weeks of meditation and made himself
available for any amount of time he was needed for interpreting. There were not many occasions for his services as
few foreigners came.

He was concerned about my not having eaten and asked
if he could take me to dinner. I was concerned about his
eating with his family, but he pushed the idea aside. I
never knew whether his life always took precedence over
the plans of his family or if to him my welfare took prece-

dence over his personal life. Or perhaps meditation took precedence over everything.

During dinner at a Chinese restaurant he spoke continually about meditation. He, too, was obviously very impressed that I had come for meditation practice and with the extremes to which I had gone to get a visa. We spoke together like old friends with some great and special interest in common.

In an hour we were back at the Center and in the Sayadaw's house. My interpreter sat beside me on the floor facing the Sayadaw.

This time I took a closer look at the Sayadaw. He sat in a large reclining chair with his feet on the chair, one knee up and the other resting on the seat. His head was shaven and he wore a saffron robe; one shoulder was bare as is the custom. He appeared to be strongly built, and his face was powerful. He must have been tall, although I never saw him standing. He seemed very young for the high esteem in which he was held, but I am a poor judge of age. He sat and listened to my interpreter relate what seemed to be the tale of my recent efforts to get a visa. The expressions on the Sayadaw's face changed frequently; his brows would knit slightly, he would smile with amusement, he would look at me in what seemed to be an effort to see who I was. When I spoke he looked directly at me. I was sure he understood English, but he always listened to a translation.

When the retelling of my visa story was over, there was a pause. And then he began to go over the practical matters of my stay. From my reading of Admiral Shattock's book, I already had some idea of what would occur and what would be expected of me. I was given my instructions: I would sit, stand, or lie for an hour concentrating only on my abdomen rising and falling during my breathing. I was to make a mental note, "Rising, falling," during each breath. The next hour I was to walk slowly about my room concentrating only on the details of my walking. I was to state verbally in my mind what was actually happening, such as, "Up, forward, down" (of my foot), or "Walking, walking," or any other verbal characterization I wished to make. After an hour of walking I was to return to the first exercise, and alternate the two exercises the entire three weeks, so far as I knew. Still more observation was prescribed. I was to watch closely *everything* I was doing, thinking, or feeling, at all times, whether I was in meditation or not. Whatever occurred within me, I was to state verbally in my mind. If a face appeared to me while I was attempting my breathing exercise, I was to verbalize in my mind, "Looking, looking," or "Seeing, seeing," until the face disappeared and I was back to observing only my breathing. If some part of my body itched, I was to say, "Itching, itching"; if I felt I had to scratch I was to scratch but not until the itching had become a distraction I could not overcome.

I knew from Shattock's book that the routine continued from 4:00 A.M. to midnight every day, so I was not surprised when this was announced. Three breaks were to occur in the day — the first meal at about 6:00 A.M., the second and last meal at about 11:00 A.M. (no food is taken after noon), and an interview with the Sayadaw in the afternoon. Otherwise, breathing and walking twenty hours each day. Back in the United States, I had wondered if I could follow such a routine, but now I was relaxed about it. In Japan I had mastered a schedule far beyond anything I would have thought I was capable of.

Before I left the house the Sayadaw said, "We hope that meditation will build a fire under you." He nodded his head, and the interview was over.

I liked the Sayadaw. He always looked directly at me as if he were examining me to see what my reactions were. I liked the humor shown in his frequent smiles and I liked his obvious concern about my long pursuit of the visa and my trip to Calcutta. I do not remember thinking of it at the time, but I suppose I assumed we would become close to each other.

The Sayadaw's assistant and my interpreter were assigned the task of getting me settled, and the three of us bowed to the Sayadaw and left.

We walked together to a discrete section of the compound where I was shown a one story, row house with six unoccupied rooms. The seventh room was inhabited by the caretaker for the house. They said I could stay here and live in any room I chose, or I could go to another part of the compound where Westerners usually stayed, a larger building across a ravine from the rest of the Center. They explained that because of the monsoons, the latter choice would involve a daily walk through the muddy ravine, but the quarters would be better. They even added a third choice: I could stay on the nearby estate of a charitable Burmese gentleman who offered residence and meals to foreign visitors. I chose the house we were in; I could see no reason to go anywhere else. I did not mind the sparseness of the furnishings and I liked the views from the windows.

The Sayadaw had left instructions that the customary meals were not to be given to me; he feared my stomach might be upset by the very simple food usually taken at the Center. They offered to have my food brought in from an hotel, or the cook would attempt to prepare something suitable for me. I said I would like to eat whatever was prepared at the Center, and the cook was brought in to discuss what I was accustomed to eating.

They spoke with the caretaker, a small, thin man of about seventy dressed in longyi and sparkling clean white shirt without collar. As they gave their instructions to him, he would glance at me, nod, and smile. From that moment on he watched over me. Whenever I walked out of my room he opened his door quietly and looked out, smiling if I smiled or very serious if I appeared to be in meditation.

The assistant and my interpreter asked me repeatedly if I had everything I needed. Seemingly satisfied that I was content, they finally left. The hour was about 6:00 P.M.

I went into my room to get settled and began my meditation practice. I do not remember being lonely. I was pleased to be there. I did not realize at the moment how tired I was.

The room was simply furnished with two beds, a table and chair, and two straw mats on the floor. One bed was prepared for my sleeping. The room was about twelve feet square and had three windows. One faced a similar house next door; the other two faced a long view of trees and grass all the way across the ravine to the larger building where the Westerners usually stayed.

The rain poured down; I shut the windows and it was warm. The rain stopped; windows open. This went on the entire evening.

I arranged my clothes on the second bed. My own bed with its sheets and mosquito netting looked inviting, but I had six hours to go before bedtime. During that time I was to read two pamphlets given me by the Sayadaw and meditate, meditate, meditate.

I changed from my summer weight, dark blue suit to sport shirt and trousers. I took off my shoes and socks; I would not wear shoes except for walking between buildings. This was the custom. The light was fading and the artificial light was small, so I started following instructions by reading the pamphlets. I was eager to get to them. As I read the longer one, I was surprised to find it was difficult; a great deal of it was Buddhist theology. I was now, I must recognize, not in a Zen school. What was stated in simple, everyday language — the heart of it, I felt — I thought I understood. The other pamphlet, which was brief, gave a list of prohibitions, but they including nothing I intended doing anyway (for example, drinking "fermented or distilled liquor and other intoxicants").

Pamphlets finished, I looked at the bed. Should I go to sleep? I wanted to follow directions and I was directed to meditate. I recalled the Zen statement, Eat when you are hungry, sleep when you are sleepy. Sleep when you are sleepy. At the moment something else had precedence and that was the meditation.

I sat down cross-legged on the straw mats and began concentrating on my breathing. Rising, falling. Rising, falling. What made me think I could sit on the floor after being unsuccessful in Japan? My ankle bones hurt almost immediately; there were no cushions here. I pulled up a chair so that it faced the wall, and I sat. There, that was better. Back to my abdomen. Thoughts about meditation, the Sayadaw's imposing face, and numerous other thoughts went through my mind and I noted them in the prescribed manner. And then I was dozing. Head up again. Back to my breathing and my abdomen. Rising, falling. Rising, falling. The Sayadaw said I could lie down to meditate; that was the solution. I lay down. Rising, falling. I fell asleep in almost no time. Awake. Lying down is no solution, simply fosters sleep. I tried walking. Up, forward, down. Up, forward, down. Eyes drooping, eyes drooping. Eyes drooping, eyes drooping. Thinking, thinking (about sleep). The evening wore on this way until midnight.

Finished with my exercises, I went to the large washroom across the hall. The caretaker looked out of his room to see if I was all right. I nodded and smiled and he returned to his room. At one end of the washroom was a huge cask of water. I took off my clothes and slowly poured the cold water over my body. Pouring, pouring. Cold, cold. Another dipper full over my body, slowly, observing what I was doing, what went through my mind, what I was feeling. I went to bed slowly, fixing attention on all my actions. Exhausted, I fell asleep immediately.

CHAPTER XIII

I F I SET MY MIND TO IT, I can usually wake up at any hour I wish. The second day I intended to awaken at four, as prescribed, but I was a half hour late. I was either so tired that my mental alarm clock was not working efficiently or I did not really want to get up. It was pitch dark and raining heavily. Water had come in the windows; I must have been so sleepy that I did not get up to close the windows when the heavy rain started. I mopped up the water with some tissues I had in my suitcase. I dressed and then washed from the great cask of water, all very slowly. The water was cold but it felt good. I began walking and then sitting. I was still dozing periodically.

I was not at any time well centered on the exercises. I was trying because I thought I had decided to try. I did not at the moment question the intensity of my motivation. I realize only now that in order to meditate as prescribed by teachers of meditation one must be very highly motivated.

The cook brought the breakfast at about 6:00 A.M. and with the help of the caretaker laid my table very quietly. I was sitting in a chair facing the wall, attempting my breathing exercise. I might as well have watched the two

men, as at the moment I was more interested in what they
were doing than I was in attending to my breathing. I
wondered what the casual, carefree cook would have prepared for me. I finally gave up my exercise and looked
around. The cook smiled, looked at me and then nodded
in the direction of the table. I remember that the food
showed he had put some thought and effort into its preparation; I find it odd that I do not recall what the food was.
Perhaps that is because I was more centered on the tastes
and visual appearance than I was in labeling the food. I
smiled and hoped to communicate my approval of his
efforts; they left. I sat by the window facing the house
next door. I ate very slowly, looking out at the wet, lush
greenery and the on and off torrential showers. Now and
then I could hear the caw of a bird. I observed my eating,
tasting the food acutely, watching my thoughts, my observations of the landscape, the odors. A month away from
my Zen meditation, I had grown accustomed to being centered on the happenings of life. Here in Burma I was supposed to add only a kind of labeling of my experiences —
tasting, tasting; hearing, hearing. Though I could do this
perfectly well, even liked it, I was not doing the more formal part well. At the time I did not even question why I
could not center on the endless walking and breathing.

The old man quietly removed the dishes as I walked. I
proceeded with the exercises, but I was sleepy a great deal
of the time.

At about 8:00 A.M. there was a momentary distraction.
I had met two college boys, an American and a Canadian,
at the hotel in Rangoon and our travel talk had come

around to my reason for being in Rangoon; it is not on the usual tourist circuit. I told them about meditation and they were immediately interested in coming to the Center. I had inquired for them and they were invited to come for a day, all the time they had to spare from their trip. They arrived, were given instructions by the Sayadaw, and were assigned rooms in my house. After a morning of meditation, we sat together eating lunch in the central hall of the house and spoke freely of meditation, college education, Burma. I do not recall noting that I would never have done this in Japan nor that this was the exact distraction about which Shattock had warned me.

Late in the afternoon my interpreter came to get me and we walked to the Sayadaw's house together.

We sat on the floor facing the Sayadaw who sat in his reclining chair.

"How does the meditation go?" was translated to me.

I said that I was very distracted, particularly by dozing. Because of what happened later, I have often wondered how he interpreted my remark. What I meant to communicate was that I was distracted during exercises; I did not mention that I was having no problem centering my attention on all other daily activities. I perhaps should have said this kind of centering was one of the outcomes of my meditation in Japan, but I did not say that. In fact, I do not recall our ever speaking about my Japanese meditation until the day I left.

The Sayadaw said that I must, of course, be very sleepy because of my hurried trip to Calcutta and my new schedule at the Center. He said simply that if I was sleepy I should sleep for a while. I did not interpret this to mean that I should sleep until I was sated. I decided I would take naps when I found it absolutely necessary.

As I was about to leave, he instructed me to continue trying.

I walked back slowly to my house, attempting to concentrate on my walking. Everything interested me. A group of dogs followed at my heels. I passed saffron-robed priests on the pathway; some would look up from their walking exercise and our eyes would meet for a second. I wondered how they were doing with their meditation: Were they frustrated? Disappointed in themselves? Were they having all the feelings I had had in Japan? I thought over my conversation with the Sayadaw. I had grown accustomed to knowing what I wanted to do and doing it. What I thought I chose to do at present was to meditate according to instructions. I had not realized that despite my good intentions, I had a need — a simple need for sleep — which distracted me and which I must take care of. To watch my distractions and recommend guards against them was the master's function in meditation, and I was glad he was there.

Walking, walking. Thinking, thinking. Walking, walking. And then a crow flew down from a roof and landed on the path a few feet ahead of me. I had never really looked at the blackness of a crow before and I stared at the shiny feathers. He cocked his head and looked at me, pecked at the wet ground, took a few hops, and flew off. Looking, looking. I should be concentrating on my walking. Walking, walking.

Back in my room, I slept for a short time and then started the breathing exercise. I had hardly begun when the two college boys came to say goodbye. I keep trying to remember whether or not I was pleased with these distractions.

The boys reported to me how difficult the meditation was, but one of them seemed to have made some progress in stilling his mind during the day. I was surprised by his progress as I had made almost no progress in Japan in the same amount of time. He had seemed to me a remarkably centered person; perhaps, I thought, people vary enormously in the difficulty they have with meditation. I had no evidence except my own experience to compare to his report, and the comparison was an interesting datum about meditation. I thought, too, about my conversation with the Burmese gentleman and his comment on Americans; perhaps he was right — Americans have the vigor and determination for meditation. I walked to the door with them and they left. They seemed to regret leaving.

I cannot say whether I was pleased they were gone or not. I suspect I was ambivalent. I really did not want to talk about meditation. Perhaps I wanted their company; maybe I was lonely, but I do not remember feeling lonely. Admiral Shattock had said, Resist the distraction of visitors. Ambivalence or not, they were gone.

Back to my instructions. Rising, falling. Rising, falling. An hour gone. Walking, walking; walking, walking. The evening wore on. My sleepiness diminished, but at midnight I was glad to go to bed.

CHAPTER XIV

ON THE THIRD DAY I was up at four. I arose slowly from the bed. I had been told that I should attempt to observe even the details of my waking in the morning, and I felt I was about ready to try that refinement of observation. I slowly lifted my body from the bed; I put my feet down slowly. I brushed my teeth, shaved, washed — observing everything. Back from the washroom to my own room, I began my exercises. Walking, walking. Walking, walking.

The morning went along uneventfully. I was by now seldom dozing. I was by no means completely centered on the exercises, but I was very much absorbed with observing everything that went on inside myself. The great simplicity of the tasks — observing my breathing and observing my walking — made them difficult to do. Counting in Japanese now seemed absorbing and easy in comparison to centering on my moving the abdomen forward and back or concentrating on my walking. I have since learned that some masters prescribe a gradual progression from a complex task to a more simple one to the simplest and most difficult of all — observation only of breathing. The effect of this procedure, which I experienced in a more recent four-day session, was to allow the student to move forward in increasingly difficult steps — from complex counting to simpler counting to the most difficult task of all, the simple observation of breathing with no counting. I believe one could say, the more complex the task, the easier to do; the simpler the task, the more difficult to do. The more there is to do, the less the distraction; the less to do, the greater the distraction. Here in Burma I was thrown immediately into the most difficult of meditation practice, or so it seems to me.

Having become through the Japanese meditation highly sensitive to everything within me and outside me, I was enjoying all of the distractions. I suppose it would be accurate to say that the distractions were what interested me most — the sounds of birds, the views from the windows, the stark room, my bathing in the cold water, the food.

During the afternoon something new occurred. I began to note numerous sensations — itches, pains, small temperature changes in my body. I had become accustomed to noting the constantly changing thoughts I had had, but the physical changes were new. I recalled my peculiar feelings in Japan, but the myriad of small physical changes had not come to my attention before. As I became more and more efficient at eliminating outside stimulation in the effort at fixing my mind on one thing, I was becoming more and more sensitive to things within myself.

I began to itch in various parts of my body — my back, then my leg, my feet, my hands. Each time the itching occurred I noted "Itching, itching" and resisted scratching. Each time, on noting the sensation repeatedly, the itching disappeared. Then minor pains arose. "Paining, paining. Paining, paining." I did not change my sitting position. The pains disappeared.

I began fully to appreciate the extent of the constantly present and constantly changing sensations and thoughts which must be occurring in me all the time. I was in the position of having to attend to them and I did. Furthermore, I was in the peculiar position of wanting to observe them and not caring if they disappeared or not. To observe was the task of the meditation. A pain comes. I observe it. I neither want it to continue nor to discontinue. I want merely to observe it until it is no longer there to observe and then I return to observing my breathing or walking.

There is a vast difference, of course, between observing *in order to* rid myself of the pain and simply observing. I do believe that once one sees the distinction, life is no longer quite the same. If I say that by observing a pain it was no longer there, I would expect you to think about trying the method *in order to* rid yourself of a pain. But in this instance your motive is different from the motive I am trying to describe.

Suppose I accept the principle that suffering is universal and expect to suffer sooner or later; suppose that this is no longer important to me. Suppose also that I accept that all things change if I do not fix them. The Zen master had said in effect: Look and see into yourself and your *inner* pains may leave. He did not say my pains would leave; he did not say they would not leave. What may happen is that I no longer care whether pains continue or cease. It may no longer be possible to care about that. If I once see that there are things that I cannot predict or change, then I can no longer concern myself with those things. And, conversely, when I know what things I can predict and if I know what to do about them, I shall be very much concerned with them.

I was supposed to be meditating. Thinking, thinking. I had a great deal to think about. My experiences in Japan alone had provided enough to think about and live with for months to come, and here in Burma even more was added. Thinking, thinking. And then I was back to my breathing. Rising, falling. Rising, falling.

In the afternoon I went again for my interview with the Sayadaw. Again he asked how I was doing with my meditation. I reported that it was going better, but that I was distracted by sensations and by thinking. I did not say what I was thinking about; he did not ask. He said that if I could not overcome distraction, I was to stop the exercises temporarily to cut the distraction — move about, scratch if it was necessary, rub myself if I was hurting. If I was thinking, I should note it in the usual way and when possible, return to my exercises.

I went back to my room and continued my meditation. To this day I keep trying to remember whether I had any foreboding of what was to happen the following morning.

CHAPTER XV

O N THE FOURTH MORNING I awoke at four, and attempted to begin my observations as soon as possible after awakening. I was doing everything slowly.

I am not sure whether it began that morning or whether in the past few days I had thought of it. Despite the intensity with which I had been watching what occurred in me I cannot remember any forewarning.

That morning I began strongly to question why I was here and whether I wanted to stay. I was not motivated, as I had been in Japan, by the challenge of trying to center my mind on exercises. I was greatly interested in trying to fix my mind on what I was doing each minute, but now that I understood the idea of it, I could practice it anywhere. I did not want to be in seclusion at the moment. I had been thinking about hundreds of things, things I *wanted* to think about, questions which had been stimulated by my experiences in Japan. I had also been distracted by my pure joy of living. While I was here to meditate, I did not really want to meditate so much as I wanted to be living normally in the world.

I walked about the room as I thought. Should I stay? I kept recalling the Sayadaw's statement: Meditation may build a fire under you. A fire under me? A fire under me. A fire had already been built in Japan, the first glimmers, shadows, and colors of which I was only beginning to see.

I thought about it over and over again. Was I avoiding something? I did not think so. Was it too hard to do? I had already mastered the rigorous schedule in Japan, and I did not find the Burmese schedule impossible, although it was more difficult. I was, of course, alone here. Was that it? Perhaps I needed people. I *have* always been gregarious; perhaps the solitude here was something I could not bear. I did not think that this explained my wanting to leave.

I felt the problem was more encompassing than these considerations. I had had an experience in Japan which I wanted to live with. I could absorb no more at this moment.

I returned to my exercises and then thought, returned again to my exercises, and again thought. By mid-morning I had made up my mind.

I would leave.

I have since wondered how long that decision would have taken if I had not previously been in meditation. I was giving up something I had planned for months.

I left my room and walked to the door. The little old man opened his door quietly and looked at me in a way that questioned whether everything was all right. Everything was all right. I smiled.

I put on my sandals at the door and walked to the assistant's tiny house, the first of a row of small houses occupied by priests in another section of the Center. Across a paved sidewalk were quarters for Burmese men in meditation. Two or three of the present group walked slowly on the central pathway in front of the houses, obviously meditating. I was walking slowly, as prescribed. I kept thinking how I could express my thoughts to the assistant and then to the Sayadaw.

The morning was damp but already quite warm; the sun shone. It was a sharply clear day, not a cloud.

I approached the assistant's house slowly. I could see him sitting on the floor near the open, unscreened windows. I walked up the steps and stood waiting outside the tiny gate on the small porch. Someone with his back to me was sitting before him. They finished speaking and the assistant dismissed the man. The assistant asked me to come in, and I moved forward and sat cross-legged on the floor in front of him. The room was barely large enough for the two of us. The room seemed warm; the priest's bare shoulder showing from his saffron robe was glistening with perspiration. His face was immobile. I began my explanation by saying that I wished to see the Sayadaw and then that I intended to leave. I must have talked for five minutes, but I could not see in his face that he understood my desire to leave. When I finished, he said merely that I would become accustomed to meditation, that I must continue trying.

We sat for a few minutes more while he discussed meditation. He explained that he had meditated at nine centers in his lifetime. Of all the methods he had tried, the

Mahasi Sayadaw's had been by far the most satisfying to him. I was sure this was his way of telling me to continue trying.

I asked, "And the state of enlightenment was achieved with each method?" I have since thought how similar my question was to that of my roommate on the last night in Japan, and the thought makes me more understanding of him.

The monk hesitated a moment. "That is one of the things we do not talk about," he said.

He reassured me that the method would come easier for me as I continued trying. I attempted no further explanation. I would have to speak to the Mahasi Sayadaw. The priest said he would take me to the Sayadaw this morning.

We arose from the floor, and as I walked on to the small porch, he said, "Stay nearby. The other American will arrive back this morning. He will want to meet you. Then all of us will go to the Sayadaw."

I remembered they had told me that an American had come nine months ago and had become a priest. I was eager to meet him.

As we stood in front of the house, the American came walking toward us from the entrance of the Center. He was a sturdy man with shaved head and dressed in a saffron robe. He and the other priest bowed to each other, hands in front as in prayer. In English the assistant introduced us, and the American gave me his large hand. He had been a teacher of Yoga in California and he gave the impression of great physical power. He had a strong face which showed the remains of suffering; at the moment he seemed relaxed. The assistant excused himself, saying that he had business to attend to. I was pleased to be with someone who might understand my leaving. It occurs to me now that the Sayadaw's assistant was probably pleased that I was with someone who might encourage my staying.

The American asked if I had seen the grounds of the Center; I replied that I had seen almost everything, except the Western quarters. We began walking across the muddy ravine toward the Western building; this was where the American had been housed during his stay at the Center.

The Western building was more imposing than any of the buildings with the exception of the Sayadaw's house. There was a long porch with numerous doors, all leading to private quarters for students. We walked to the end of the porch, passed through a screen door, and we were in his room. He pointed out that this was the same room Admiral Shattock had used when he was there. The room had a personal touch and also the great luxury of screens on the door and windows. I joked about the lavishness of his quarters as opposed to my own. It was a casual comment, the kind of thing one American might say to another. Hours later, I wondered if this was the comment which caused the thing that happened later.

Conversation came easily. There seemed to be no barriers between us. We spoke about meditation practices and I told him about my experiences in Japan. He listened with intense interest. And then I told him that I was leaving the Burmese Center. I wondered what he would say; I did not have to wait for a reply.

Without hesitation he said, "Of course you should leave. With the intensity of the experience you had in Japan, you cannot possibly meditate so strenuously this soon again."

I told him the assistant did not understand this, and I asked if he would help me explain to the Sayadaw my reasons for leaving. I do not recall his answer; perhaps he did not reply.

He did say we would both be having interviews with the Mahasi Sayadaw this morning; he confided that he was leaving the priesthood. He said his meditation with the Sayadaw had been the most profound experience of his life; now he was going to teach meditation in the United States or in France. His interview this morning would be a formal de-robing from the priesthood. I wondered if I would be in the room during the ceremony; it interested me, but I was sure it would be private. I did not have a chance to ask him; as we stood talking, the assistant came to get us for our interviews.

The interpreter was already in the room when we arrived. He was sitting on the floor near the Sayadaw, some distance from where I would be sitting. Someone must have telephoned him to come. He nodded to me and smiled as I bowed to the Sayadaw and took my position on the floor across from them. The American, too, bowed and sat on the floor before the Sayadaw. He and the Sayadaw laughed and spoke together only as people can when they know each other well. I was not included in the conversation.

There was a short silence and then the Sayadaw turned

to me. I felt awkward in beginning. I wondered what my interpreter would think; perhaps he already knew. When I first arrived at the Center, the Sayadaw had told me a story about a German couple who had come for meditation and after a couple of days had disappeared without a word about leaving. Just four days ago we had laughed together about the story.

I finished my explanation and waited. The Sayadaw, too, paused a second. He looked at me intently and then said that meditation was difficult and I must continue trying. The American sat quietly, not raising his eyes. I wanted the Sayadaw to understand my reasons for leaving; I wanted to leave him with a decent opinion of me and of Americans. I was getting nowhere. I decided to use his own words because I thought they were appropriate; I said he had hoped a fire might be set in meditation: such a thing had happened to me in Japan, and I was not motivated to meditate so strenuously now.

The Sayadaw's face seemed to change. I felt he had finally realized that I would leave, that it was settled.

After a pause, he asked, "Do you understand the changing nature of all things?"

I said that I had arrived at this understanding in Japan and that I had seen it in a new way yesterday. I was referring to the coming and going of thoughts and sensations.

I did not expect what came next. The Sayadaw said, "You mean you understood it with your mind. As far as we are concerned, you have reached the first stage and there are eighteen stages." I gave no reply because there was none. I was angry.

There was another pause and he said, "The Zen method is altogether different. Ours is the method prescribed by the Buddha. You may have succeeded in the Zen method, but you may not say you have succeeded in ours. And do not tell people our method is like Zen."

I replied that I had no intention of telling anyone these things.

There was another pause. The Sayadaw and I sat looking at each other. Then he said, "At least you were good enough to tell us of your intention to leave. You did not run away like the German woman and her husband."

I did not expect this last reference. My face flushed with anger.

The interview was over. I could not find words to say anything more on the subject. The misunderstanding was too deep to continue the conversation. I felt alone, shut out from any chance at communication, frustrated and angry. I thanked him for the kindness shown to me during my stay and said that I should like to return when I was ready for more meditation. I do not remember his reply.

He turned to the other American. No one asked me to leave and I did not rise to go without a sign from the Sayadaw.

The de-robing ceremony began. The ritual instructions by the Sayadaw were given with great seriousness. The American did what he was told, for the most part repeating over and over again that he was leaving the priesthood and was now a layman. Tears rolled down his cheeks. The tears were interspersed with laughter at small, inconsequential occurrences which I do not remember. This

mixing of humor with seriousness was a quality I saw repeatedly in people who engage in meditation. Perhaps we
can see humor in all kinds of things when we gain enough
perspective on life and on ourselves.

The American changed into his Western clothes—a
part of the ritual. The short ceremony was over. The
American and I bowed to the Sayadaw and we left. When
we were outside, the American said he would like to continue our conversation but that he had to visit friends in
the city. We exchanged addresses and said we would write
to each other. Nothing was said by either of us about our
interviews.

I walked back alone to my house. I was still angry.
Days later I realized that I had developed a new ability to
allow myself honest indignation and anger when that was
what I was really feeling.

As I walked, I went over the interview in my mind.
There had been no time for the Sayadaw to know how I
felt or what I had experienced. He had asked me a question about what I understood and I had answered him, and
then he had told me what I *really* understood. How often
I had heard psychotherapists use this kind of dichotomy—
the dichotomy between "intellectual understanding" and
"feeling." And how often I had been angered by it. How
presumptuous we are to tell another person how he feels or
what he understands; we can never know this about another person.

I wondered how he could think I would profess that I
had "succeeded" in his method when I did not even know
what he might mean by "succeeded." Perhaps his experi-

ences with Westerners had been unfortunate, but why must he generalize to me, a particular Westerner?

To point out how good I was to announce my departure was preposterous to me. I was his guest and student and I would have told him whatever he wanted to know about me. But then how could he know what to expect of me? How could he know anything about me?

I remained frustrated and increasingly angry. I liked him and wanted him to like me. I wanted us to understand each other. And I had no way to accomplish either goal.

Returning to my room, I packed my belongings. Once again I looked out at the views from the windows — the house next door, the green countryside, the muddy ravine, the Western building. The sun had disappeared; the sky had become clouded over and gray.

The cook and the little old man came to my room and carried my bags to a small car owned by the Center. As they put my bags in the back of the car, the assistant appeared. He looked at my bags and said something to the cook. He then turned to me and said that the car was not available for transportation at the moment. I asked him about the charges for my stay and paid what he calculated, a very small sum. He assigned the cook to accompany me to the main road and to find a cab for me.

The sky was full of clouds. It had begun to rain. I raised my umbrella, and as we walked together I tried to shield both of us. I wanted to say something to him, to share the experience of this morning, but that would not have been appropriate. He probably already knew what had happened. And besides, we did not speak the same language.

We waited together on the main road. It was raining heavily by now; cars had pulled up under trees for protection from the downpour. Finally a small cab came racing along and the cook hailed it. He put my bags in the cab and directed the driver to my hotel. I huddled up on one of the two benches in the small passenger section behind the driver. The canvas sides of the cab flapped in the wind and rain poured in on me and my luggage. As the cab moved off, I looked back. The cook stood in the rain, smiling and waving to me.

CHAPTER XVI

D RENCHED, I was soon back in the hotel in the middle of town. I could not get my old room with the view of the main street. The desk clerk, who knew me by now, apologized and explained that the only room left was in the center of the hotel. I went upstairs, into the room, and opened the shuttered window. There was a view only of the blank side wall of the building next door. I had to shut the window quickly as it was still raining heavily.

I changed into dry clothes, washed my hands and face, combed my hair, and went downstairs to the dining room to call my American friends. Over the phone I said only that I had left the Center; perhaps my voice revealed more than that. In another half hour a car was sent to take me to have lunch with them.

At lunch I spilled out my morning's experience and my feelings. They listened attentively, and I was glad that they made no comments. They had spent many years in the Far East, too many years to make quick statements about misunderstandings between East and West.

I realized I could not leave things the way they stood. From my friends' home I called the two Burmese men who had almost become friends, the two previous ministers of the government who had helped me and talked to me about meditation. In some communities, news spreads fast and I knew both of them would soon know I had left the Center. I felt both men would be as perplexed as I was angry. I wondered if we could understand each other. If I could arrange interviews with them, I would try again to explain myself. Perhaps they would understand—and perhaps they would make the Sayadaw understand. By telephone I asked both of them for interviews the following day.

Early the next day I went to see each man in his own home. Both men were in poor health. The two interviews went much the same way. While they seemed cool at first, both men changed as we spoke. Whatever it was that seemed to change their impression, they both became more sympathetic and said they hoped I would return.

My American friends' chauffeur helped me pick up my bags at the hotel and drove me to their house for lunch. There were other guests, and I could do nothing but report that my interviews had gone well. I felt at home. I had temporarily forgotten my interview with the Sayadaw and today's interviews.

No one came to the airport with me. My American friends were busy with afternoon diplomatic duties. Neither of my two Burmese helpers were well enough to see me off.

From the window of the plane I looked down at Rangoon and its heavy, wet greenery. The rain had stopped by now and everything was lit by the sun. Sitting back in my window seat I began thinking about my interviews today.

Neither of the two men had said very much, but I now remembered references to the possibility that I was not comfortable in the Center, that I did not find the living accommodations suitable. At those moments I must have ignored the idea; it had never occurred to me. I wondered whether this kind of misunderstanding could have been the basis of the Sayadaw's remarks to me, but I doubted it. It even occurred to me that the American priest might have relayed to the Sayadaw my comment about his lavish quarters, but I was sure he had not, and I could not believe there had been time prior to my interview for him to speak about such an incidental comment.

No, there was something deeper than any of that. It was, I felt, an unfortunate misunderstanding between Easterner and Westerner. I had been lucky that there had been no previous misunderstanding of any magnitude during any of my time in the Far East. The Sayadaw had had some unfortunate experiences with Westerners; there must have been more than the incident with the German couple. We did not speak the same language, and that is often an insuperable barrier. Language is always a potential problem until someone learns the other's language; it had been my responsibility to learn Burmese. Customs and manners can always be a problem, to be solved only by living a long time in the other's country. Prejudice of one sort or another can always be a problem until each person meets and comes to know more than a few people of the other culture. Perhaps with all the barriers, it is a miracle that profound understanding and respect and help can ever be reached.

The Sayadaw's comparisons of his method to those of Zen were not an unusual phenomenon; I was accustomed to constant comparisons of psychological methods. I also knew that when comparisons are based on unstated and therefore unagreed upon goals, they are almost always unfortunate, especially when value judgment is their foundation and their function. I wanted him to be above such comparisons, but that was my problem — the endless problem of wanting the people we like or admire to fit into our own perfectionistic ideals. For him to call on authority, in this case the authority of Buddha, is common enough; throughout my life I had heard misunderstandings further confused by hailing a great religious or philosophical figure to stand on our side.

I wondered how my experience in Burma would have seemed to me if I had not been in Japan. Would I have stayed in meditation? Probably, but I do not really know.

I have only realized very recently that when I tell friends about my experiences in Japan and Burma, they always refer to my "failure" in Burma. They always try to explain the "failure" — "Jack, you are too gregarious to be left alone like that. You needed people around you as you had in Japan." "It was too hard and too long to carry through." "You must have been exhausted by that time."

I realize only now that I have never considered leaving the Burmese Center a failure. I have never even found the Japanese Roshi's word "succeeding" really palatable to me. Perhaps it was meditation that allowed me not to see things in this way. When we chain ourselves with notions of what we *must* have happen, we lose what *does* happen.

When we free ourselves to accept what does happen, we might even allow ourselves to appreciate it and live it fully. I believe meditation is one method of seeing that crucial distinction.

I realize only now that my decision to leave was made more quickly than I could ever before have made such a decision. Big decisions never come easily for me. I suppose behind my decision was the realization by the time I was in the Burmese Center that I had changed and that the task had changed for me. I was certainly responding to the conditions of the moment and not to carefully laid plans. That is the point after all.

Would it have been better if I had not gone to Burma? I increasingly appreciate my short time there. The experience added another dimension to meditation for me. To the extent that I initially had a goal, it was to see first-hand some of the ancient methods used in the Far East to help man. If I had gone only to Japan, I believe I would have come home believing that there was a method of great significance, but I would have felt it existed only in Japan and only with the Roshi. Instead I feel that in Burma there is also something of deep meaning, and if this is true, meditation practices in many centers must have methods of profound value.

The summer had turned out strangely. I could not possibly have predicted what actually happened. But then we seldom can.

EPILOGUE

Perhaps the feelings and insights resulting from experiences of this nature are not communicable. Personal insights of deep meaning are generally, it seems, very simple and when stated, usually mean little or nothing or seem obvious to the reader. Perhaps anything of a profound influence on a human being can only be seen in its effects on a thousand daily events. These are not in my power to show beyond the attempts I have already made. I can, however, make some generalizations which I believe should be made.

Even when I was quite young — I suppose from the time I was old enough to compare and conceptualize — I used to try to generalize about life and people, the way children do, especially when they are unhappy. I do not believe I was really a disturbed child, but I remember being very unhappy at times. At about eleven I had a startling insight: that people actually change. It was, I suppose, the kind of insight which comes of desperation. I remember that the words quite startled me: people change. I had wanted desperately for things to be different, for other people to be different, and for me to be different. I suppose that from a temporary sense of endless unhappiness I had assumed that people never change.

I do not remember my early insight having any influence on me as a psychologist. In fact, I was, as a graduate psychology student, influenced in quite the opposite way. I was taught — though it was never quite stated this way — that people do not change in any fundamental way; that once a schizophrenic, always a schizophrenic; once this or that, little can happen to change the "basic structure." If for some reason change did occur, it was not "deep" unless it was brought about by years of psychoanalysis. "Ordinary psychotherapy," the kind that is done on a once a week basis and for periods of a year or less, might solve a problem but the patient remained essentially the same, I was taught.

Never one to be satisfied with what I am taught, always seeking some new view of things, I looked about me and saw people changing remarkably — with and without psychoanalysis. I wondered what "deep" change meant, and my conclusion was that we must consider a real change to be something which enables a person to move in the direction he wishes to go and away from immobilization, enables him to stop the repetition of old and unsatisfying patterns, and to cease being his own worst enemy. I saw these life remolding changes in some of my friends who were being analyzed — and in others who were not being analyzed. I also saw other changes, changes which seemed to be related only to fortuitous factors; at least this is what people reported to me.

I think we must take seriously the reports of people

when they give the reasons for great changes in their lives. We often act as if only our own personal theory will give the real reason other people change. Researchers have divided groups of mental hospital patients, given half of them some form of therapy and left the others alone, and report that a given percentage of *both* groups get better. Where we fail is in not asking both groups why they changed. We often act as if people know nothing about themselves.

I have no question about the great changes my own psychoanalysis helped me bring about in myself. My friends report great changes in themselves as a result of their psychoanalysis, and I can see the changes in them. In my work as a psychotherapist I have never been given the time to see people over long periods as occurs in psychoanalysis. Nevertheless, I have seen deep changes in some of my short-term patients; and I assumed that some of the changes were related to our therapy together. At least this is what patients report. Patients have told me, in follow-up interviews long after therapy was over, that a single statement from me changed their lives. When I ask in surprise what the statement was, I frequently find that I never made such a statement — in fact, I do not even think in the terms they use. I had harbored a totally different idea, my idea, of why they changed. Sometimes I see no change at all and discover that the patient is experiencing all kinds of changes.

I know people who have been in great distress, on the point of suicide, who make up their minds to change their lives and then change by what appears to be sheer effort.

Remarkable changes result from chemotherapy. Also reported are unusual changes resulting from the so-called psychedelic drugs. We hear of remarkable changes resulting from various kinds of religious experiences. And then there are changes reported from seemingly chance factors. A friend happens to meet the right employer and it changes his life and it changes him. A man full of problems marries a woman no one would have predicted he would marry, the "wrong" woman for him, and becomes an increasingly productive person.

Psychologists place little store by fortuitous factors, and religion for them is not a currently popular topic. Modes change, of course. In American psychology of years past, William James chose religion as the subject for one of his major works. The word meditation has a religious ring about it, and one wonders, because of this, how long it will be before any real psychological interest will be shown in the subject.

Meditation, as I experienced it, was not an occult or "spiritual" phenomenon. It was not religious in any of the usual senses of the word. On the other hand, it was not disparate with any of the mature religions I am familiar with.

I took no drugs, no mescaline, no LSD, no psilocybin. I found no savior. I did, however, have teachers. The teacher's function in both situations was to aid me in the avoidance of distraction — from the distraction of an uncomfortable sitting position to the distraction of fear when unusual phenomena occurred. The teacher was not there as a positive aid in any way; he could produce nothing for me. Whatever was to be derived was my responsibility and only mine.

I have wondered about the long-range results of meditation as compared with those changes produced by an outside agent such as a drug. I think there might be great differences between the two effects. The effect on me of what *I* produce may be very different from the effect on me of insights produced by an outside agent.

The implications of meditation on the whole problem of control of man's behavior extend, unfortunately, beyond man's control of his own behavior to man's control of the behavior of others. I believe the isolation and sensory deprivation experiments of great current interest are also of great moment. I believe the results of these experiments will be used more and more for man's inhumanity to man. As we learn more about isolation and depriving man of stimulation, we may come to use it to force individual men to perform acts against their "will." The obvious implications for war and national security measures are myriad and of the highest importance to a nation.

A study of meditation might be conceived as an extension of studies of isolation (it would, approached from various angles, be much more than that, I believe). It seems very apparent to me that when we learn how, through isolation and sensory deprivation, to "break a man down," we will then be looking frantically for safeguards against the effects of such treatment. No nation heavily dependent upon security of intelligence can risk the use of psychological methods on its human storehouses of intelligence without seeking methods to insure against the leak of its intelligence. Such an insurance may exist in meditation.

Meditation in one form or another is practiced throughout the world, and the forms of meditation are apparently myriad. During that summer and since then I have spoken with many people about meditation practices and have begun to grasp the range of subject matter used in meditation. Besides the methods I used — the breathing and walking taught by the Sayadaw and the numbers and word (MU) taught by the Roshi, one may center on an abstract concept, a word such as "love" or a sentence such as "Nothing remains the same." Instead of the moving abdomen, one may concentrate on an unmoving part of the body such as the center of the forehead. One may center on a koan, a kind of riddle, given by the teacher, or on one's own central problem of the moment. One may even have no subject matter at all but simply "think"; one may even attempt not to think. Changes, major and minor, are reported as the result of all these methods.

I would like to see us address ourselves directly to the question of what produces changes in people. I would like to see us use all kinds of information, including the data from the Far Eastern methods of producing change. I think the day will come when we will do just that.

I have given a great deal of thought to the difference in the Roshi's method and the method of the Sayadaw. Whether or not I could have stood the solitude in Burma I do not know, but it is worth speculating about. I believe that doing alone something so strenuous as the Burmese meditation would be terribly difficult for anyone. This is, I believe, due not only to the solitary nature of the situation but also to the lack of variation in exercises. The less the variation, the greater the monotony. The greater the monotony, the greater the distraction. The more intense the distraction, the longer the time required to fix the mind fully on the task. The Roshi, it seems to me, solved the solitude problem by making meditation a group process in which people motivate each other by their very presence. He solved the monotony problem by introducing subtle but enormous variation in exercises.

I cannot say what the Burmese meditation system produces, but my guess is that overcoming the lack of encouragement and overcoming the monotony are feats which, once mastered, must produce something of great meaning. Exactly what that is I cannot say because I did not experience it.

I find it interesting to speculate on a question and a doubt which arises every time I mention a five-day course of meditation. People wonder what such a short effort could produce; most people familiar in any way with Far Eastern meditation practices doubt that a mere five days could produce anything at all. Tens of thousands of American people attend religious retreats during which some form of meditation is undertaken, but somehow we never compare these with what we hear of Far Eastern meditation. Perhaps because of the endless years used in meditation by some Easterners, our expectations are different. If a great change occurs in a very short period, we are doubtful about it. Maybe we are doubtful because we are taught that the good things of life come only through suffering and hard work, both of considerable duration. As I have already suggested, we have grave doubts about the possibility of deep changes occurring in short-term therapy or as the result of a fortuitous event.

These questions and doubts may be related in part to the problem of perception of Time. How long is a moment? How short is a year? A man meditates for eighteen years and at one particular moment something happens to him which changes his life. Another man meditates for five days and on the fifth day something happens which changes his life. Perhaps the changes are not comparable, but perhaps they are. Perhaps the difference in methods can be found to account for the differences in time required to realize a change. We find the same kinds of time differences in psychotherapy; here too we might consider differences in method. We must, of course, always consider the matter of readiness. It could be that I was uniquely ready for meditation at the time I practiced it.

Long ago I discovered as a psychologist that to listen to someone is to listen carefully to what *is* said and observe closely what is not said. Neither the Roshi nor the Sayadaw said, We will discuss whatever you choose to discuss and together we will work out something very important to you. They did not say, Behave differently and you will solve your problems. They said none of these things; in fact they did not even allude to them. No problem was ever stated. And they said nothing about having any role in any part of what might occur.

The Roshi by implication minimally described "mental

health" (that is my term, not his) — absence of "inner" pain and a view of one's "unconditional nature." It is true that he vaguely characterized the feeling of inner pain and equally vaguely characterized unconditional nature. He did not give the terms any content, however; that was for me to do. He said in very vague terms that there was a goal, and I had only the vaguest feeling for what he alluded to. The only content in the goal of meditation was to rid myself of inner pain and see my unconditional nature so that I might use it. I think I am honest in saying that his words did not make me hope for or work toward any goal of grand proportions or even a change that would have significance to my life. I had, however, strong motivation to perform the very concrete tasks the Roshi gave me to do. By the time I arrived in Japan, I had worked through all of my doubts and fears and was ready to do whatever was asked of me. The Roshi gave me sounds to make and told me to listen only to them. Furthermore, he implied that this was possible for me to do.

Neither teacher stated what form my relationships should take or what form any of my life should take. Nothing was even remotely alluded to as "bad" except inner pains. I was taught a *method* of an extremely concrete nature, not an attitude toward life. Whatever changes in attitude there were came from me.

Both teachers were in essence saying, Do this very specific thing; it is very hard to do, but try your best; and there is a chance that you will get a glimpse of something, but I will not (indeed cannot?) tell you what that is.

No stencil of interpretations (or value statements) was

provided to place on my experiences to judge them. I did not label one action aggressive and another passive, one part of me id and another part ego, one part my real self and another my ideal self, or put any other conceptual labels on anything about me or my experiences. While I was told by the Sayadaw to label my observations — thinking, feeling, itching, seeing — there was no hint of dividing the mind or me into parts. The Roshi referred to the conditional and unconditional as, incidentally, does the Western philosopher, Martin Buber. This conceptualization is not the same as conceptualizing a real self and an ideal self. Neither is it the same as conceptualizing a conscious mind and an unconscious mind, or a conscious self and an unconscious self.

Nothing was said by either teacher about conscious or unconscious. Perhaps there is no mention of unconscious because the masters of meditation knew centuries ago that everything is there to look at if we address ourselves to it. The very essence of meditation is, after all, to see, to center on, what is going on within oneself.

What occurs is that the meditator observes the everchanging nature of himself and of everything else. Once one sees that, it is then impossible to speak of what I *always* do, or *never* do. Labels implying permanent qualities have no more meaning.

We limit ourselves endlessly by notions of what we are, as if we were fixed forever, as if we were things. We have a million limiting labels to prevent us from seeing what we might do with ourselves. We are "neurotic"; he is "psychotic." She is "frigid"; he is "a homosexual." We are

"obsessive"; she is "an hysteric." And how these labels
hold us back from realizing our capacities is staggering to
think about.

Besides fixing people forever and unchangingly with
these labels, we also eliminate from our minds the qualities
not included in the labels. We see only the neurotic ele-
ments (whatever that might mean) in ourselves and
others, and we eliminate everything not included in the
labels. We need only look at psychological and psychiatric
reports to see our great emphasis on qualities included in
labels. These pitfalls are present not only in our view of
others but in our view of ourselves.

In a way it seems a shame to me that I could not have
gone to Burma first. It would have been an experiment the
results of which would interest me enormously. My question is, Would I have gained any intensely meaningful
change in my outlook in Burma, considering that I may
have been expecting something after reading Shattock's
book? My guess is that I would not have had a deeply
meaningful experience, at least not in three weeks. I believe the vague expectations supplied by Shattock's book
might have interfered with my progress. To expect something from an experience is often to hope that the experience will do something to me, not that *I* will make it something of importance. In meditation no one did anything to
me; whatever was done, I did. I am certain that the expectations one may have from meditation comprise one of the
reasons the Sayadaw requires the participant to come for
ten weeks. To get over the idea that something will happen *to* me by something imposed on me takes a very long

time if I once expect it. The same thing occurs in psycho-therapy. How much time must be wasted in the patient's waiting for the therapist to do something to him! And how much time must be wasted by the unskilled therapist in trying to do something to the patient!

In therapy, concentration is often centered on a goal; in meditation my concentration was on a method or process. Concentrating on a goal instead of the process is like wait-ing for the future or worrying about what *will* happen rather than living now and appreciating what *is* happen-ing. The Existential therapists I know personally seem to be talking about this idea, but they always seem to fall into the trap of thinking about long-term goals (*their* goals) for the patient.

I keep wondering whether the whole idea of goal-directed therapy is a mistaken one. Perhaps we are most effective as therapists when we center our attention on what the patient is saying now, what problems he has *now*, and leave the choice of the ever-changing goals to him.

I believe that in the best of therapy the issue of where lies the responsibility for choice and action is clear. Be-cause of the traditional status of therapists as healers, how-ever, the issue of responsibility in therapy is often a cloudy one. The psychotherapist is apt to assume responsibility for choices and action that are the right and responsibility of the patient alone. In my meditation experiences there was no indication that the teacher was a healer; the idea was not even mentioned. I was the only healer for me. In meditation I was to see *alone* whatever I saw. The choice was mine. The action was mine.

The training requires intense discipline. I have at times entertained the notion that the experiences were only that — train in self discipline. Certainly we in the West have a thousand ways to avoid recognizing our part in what happens to us and other people. Not the least of our ways of avoidance is our use of the idea of The Unconscious; if we can blame our actions on The Unconscious we need assume no responsibility for them.

Discipline seems to have become a pejorative word to us in the West. It connotes to many of us the rigidity of a Nazi soldier, the "compulsive" nature of a "neurotic," something that is "bad" for our children. We have forgotten its positive quality. We have lost respect for demanding things of ourselves, taking the responsibility for making the most of ourselves through sheer effort — discipline.

In meditation I got a glimpse of what I am in control of and what is outside my control — and how much I am in control in various situations and how much some other person or factor has the control. What I also learned was this: What *I* am in control of for *me* is far beyond anything I would have dreamed of. This is not unlike saying that my capabilities in every way are perhaps endless. The Yogis have for centuries demonstrated the vast capacities of man. I had been taught and had come to believe they were finite; perhaps they are in fact infinite.

Somehow through the experiences, perhaps through the discipline I saw myself capable of, I learned a new kind of self respect — and the expected increase of respect for others. By respect I mean concern for what we are capable of experiencing. If I become respectful of what I *could* be doing, I become more sensitive to the kinds of stimuli I give my attention and time to. And I can avoid stimuli — from specific magazines to specific people — which for me produce nothing but confusion and displeasure.

I do not believe that meditation will solve the mental illnesses of the world. Meditation is not for everyone but then neither is psychoanalysis. It is not, I suspect, for the very seriously disturbed person, or even the person who is lost for the moment; it is not for the person who wishes no deep self-study and insight. I doubt if it should be practiced by even the moderately ill. It is not even for all those whose personal problems are manageable. Some people who have interesting and satisfying work, deep relationships with other people, and who are getting what they want from life may never want to experience the difficulties, or even gain the possible rewards, of meditation. I do not believe most people would attempt it or go through even one day of it. It is too hard. Motivation must be higher than most of us have for self-realization. But then that is true of long-term therapy too.

Meditation may be, however, for two states of mind. The first is the attitude of the explorer — the person interested in experiences of all kinds, the person who wants to see more than he has seen, who wants to explore the mind. Meditation may also be for those who believe or feel that there is experience beyond a deeply satisfying life work, beyond warm and meaningful personal relationships, beyond the pleasures life ordinarily provides most of us. There was a little of both of these attitudes in me at the time I left the United States.

My friends ask, Did your experiences in meditation change your psychological practice? Meditation changed my functioning as both a diagnostician and as a therapist. I saw the changes, the constant changes, which occurred in me second by second, and that view into oneself can change one's whole view of life. I no longer see people as fixed, as a category, an unchanging entity. I no longer see people as unmoved by fortuitous factors. I no longer see myself as single-handedly helping a patient change himself; he is changing himself constantly as a result of all his life experiences only one small part of which is his contact with me.

I believe that the great experience of seeing, second by second, changes so clearly and repeatedly in myself, demonstrated to me that change is everywhere. I cannot, since I am not God, make definite predictions about myself or anyone else, because change and chance are everywhere. I cannot tell anyone what to do because being unable to predict anything with deep and, I think, foolish assurance, I cannot decide what another human being should do. I can talk to someone about his problems and the possible solutions, and he may gain perspective, but he and chance will have to take over from there. I can only sit by, searching my mind for new ideas for him to consider, watching myself to be sure I am honest and that I do not fall into the dark trap of thinking I know what he should do. I can only sit by, anxious about the slings and arrows of his life, hopeful that he gets what he wants, while the patient makes his own life choices, for it is he and he alone who knows everything that can be known. I can only guess what thoughts he has had; he knows. I can only guess at the outcome of his choices; it is he, not I, who must make them and live them. It is he who must make the effort and he who must suffer the consequences of benevolent and destructive chance.

The status of meditation in the Eastern countries is somewhat like the status of psychotherapy and psycho-analysis in the West. I met very few people in the Far East who knew anything beyond the bare essential facts about meditation. I found high respect for those who engage in it, but also the wide opinion that it is too hard to do. I suppose I should not be surprised by the reaction I hear in the United States when meditation is mentioned. Interest-ing, people say, but too odd. Most of us do not find it odd that people for years on end pay another human being great sums of money to listen to their problems and make a response. In the East I spoke to a group of graduate psy-chology students to whom I asked the question, Would you have psychoanalysis if it were offered to you free? Not one of them wanted any part of it. Meditation in the East and psychotherapy in the West seem to have in common the same response from the cultures of which they are a part — a difficult process with the possibility of bringing great changes in the life of the participant.

Perhaps some day the people of our two cultures will open themselves to the methods of helping people which each has found deeply meaningful. Eastern psychologists have gone in that direction by exposing themselves to our methods and points of view. I can only hope that we will open ourselves to what the Far East has to offer us. In my opinion, meditation is unquestionably an offering of large proportions.

We have many notions of what produces change in people, but few of us study change or even open ourselves to change in our own outlook. We have a million ways of resisting change but it is inevitable, and how dull life would be if that were not true.